Prolegomena to Research Methodology

Prolegomena to Research Methodology

Prof. Dr. G Devarajan
UGC Emeritus Fellow
Dept.of Library & Information Science
University of Kerala, Trivandrum

Ess Ess Publications
New Delhi

Prolegomena to Research Methodology

ISBN: 978-81-7000-639-8

Rs.450/-

First Published 2011

Published by:
Ess Ess Publications
4837/24, Ansari Road,
Darya Ganj,
New Delhi-110 002.
INDIA
Phones: 23260807, 41563444
Fax: 41563334
E-mail: info@essessreference.com
www.essessreference.com

Cover Design by *Patch Creative Unit*

Printed and bound in India at Salasar Imaging Systems.

Dedicated to my parents
(Late) Shri. Pavoor S Janardhanan
and
Smt.Leksmy

Contents

Preface

There is no alternative to truth and therefore to research. The purpose of research is to discover answers to questions through the application of scientific procedures. These activities pave ways for the development of nascent knowledge and development of knowledge infrastructure and knowledge reservoir for societal development.

Research methodology, a critical component of training for any research programme, seldom receives the attention it deserves in most academic institutions in India. Methodologies are often conflated with methods and techniques of data analysis. with limited understanding of the logic underlying the various techniques and methods. This book contains nine chapters discussing the various aspects or systematic procedures in research such as the concept of research, scientific method of research, hypotheses, areas of research, data collection and sampling, research methods and tools, report writing, evaluation of research reports etc. Also, systematic procedures for the preparation of a project proposal with suitable examples are given. The author believes that the book will be useful to students and teachers in Social Science and management disciplines in general and of Library and Information Science disciple in particular.

The author records his great appreciation and hearty thanks to Mr.Sumit Sethi, M/s Ess Ess Publications, New Delhi in bringing out this book in good format within record time.

Prof.Dr.G.Devarajan

Thiruvananthapuram

01.06.2011

1

The Concept of Research

INTRODUCTION

The word research is derived from the French 'recherché' from rechercher, to search closely. Chercher means to search. The word "Research" means repeated search or repeated inquiry. Research can be defined as the search for knowledge or any systematic investigation to establish facts. It is a voyage in the sea of knowledge. It is a movement from known to the unknown frontiers of knowledge. In fact, research is an art of scientific investigation. It is a structured enquiry that utilizes acceptable scientific methodology to solve problems and create new knowledge that is generally applicable. It is a conscious and planned activity devoted to investigation of a phenomenon with the objective of expanding the frontiers of existing knowledge.

According to Random House dictionary of English language, research is a systematic inquiry into a subject in order to revise facts theories etc. Webster's Third International dictionary of English language defines research as "studious inquiry or examination, especially critical or exhaustive investigation or experimentation having for its aim the discovery of new facts, and their correct interpretation, the revision of accepted conclusions, theories or laws in the light of newly discovered facts, or practical applications of new or revised conclusions, theories or laws". The Advanced Learners' Dictionary of Current English states the meaning of research as "careful investigation or inquiry specially through search for new facts in any branch of knowledge" According to the Random House Dictionary, Research is a systematic inquiry into a subject in order to discover or revise facts, theories, etc. Encyclopedia of social science defines research as "the manipulation of things, concepts or symbols for the purpose of generalization to extend, correct or verify knowledge whether that knowledge aids in the construction of theory or in practice of an art"

Charles H Busha and Stephen P Harter define research 'as a systematic quest for knowledge that is characterized by disciplined enquiry. Efficient and effective approach to expand knowledge in the conduct of special, planned and structured investigations" Redman and Mory define research as a "Systematised effort to gain new knowledge" Best and Kahn define research' as the systematic and objective analysis and recording of controlled observations that may lead to the development of generalization, principles or theories, resulting in prediction and possibly ultimate control of events" Emory defines 'research as any organized inquiry designed and carried out to provide information for solving a problem.'. Dr.S.R.Ranganathan describes research as representing a critical and exhaustive investigation to discover new facts, to interpret them in the light of the newly discovered facts and to apply the conclusion to practical purpose. According to Clifford Woody research comprises defining and redefining problems, formulating hypothesis or suggested solutions; collecting, organizing and evaluating data; making deductions and reaching conclusions; and at last carefully testing the conclusions to determine whether they fit the formulating hypothesis. Kerlinger defines research as a 'systematic, controlled, empirical and critical investigation of hypothetical propositions about the presumed relations among natural phenomena' Pauline V Young defines research as ' a scientific undertaking which, by means of logical and systematic techniques, aims to : i) discover new facts or verify and test old facts, ii) analyse their sequences, interrelationships and causal explanations, iii) develop new scientific tools, concepts and theories which would facilitate reliable and valid study of human behaviour.

J.H Shera defines research as ' an intellectual process whereby a problem is perceived, divided into its constituent elements, and analysed in the light of certain basic assumptions: valid and relevant data are collected ; hypotheses (if any), are through objective testing rejected, amended, or proved. The generalisable results of this process, qualify as principles, laws or truths, that contribute to man's understanding of himself, his works or his environment'. In fact research is an intellectual, careful ordered, reflective, and a systematic attempt to discover new facts or sets of facts, or new relationships among facts.

PM Cook outlines research as an honest, exhaustive, intelligent searching for facts and their meanings or implications, with reference to a problem. According to him each letter in the word RESEARCH stands for specific aspect as detailed below:

R = Rational way of thinking

E = Expert and Exhaustive treatment

S = Search and Solution

E = Exactness

A = Analysis

R = Relationship of facts

C = Critical observation, Careful planning, Constructive attitude and Condensed generalisation

H = Honesty and Hard working.

CHARACTERISTICS OF RESEARCH

An analytical approach to the above definitions brings out the attributes or characteristics of research as:

i) It is a scientific and studious inquiry;

ii) An intellectual activity of higher order

iii) An investigation of a phenomenon, event or activity

iv) Aims to discover data and facts and their interpretations

v) To arrive at conclusions to formulate new theories, and laws or revise the already established theories and laws;

vi) To be accepted or rejected to the already existing general pool of knowledge.

Good V Carter underlines the following characteristics of research.

- Research is a systematic and critical investigation into a phenomena.
- It is not a mere compilation, but a purposive investigation; it aims at describing, interpreting and explaining a phenomenon.
- It adopts scientific method.
- It is objective and logical, applying possible tests to validate the measuring tools and the conclusions

reached.

- It is based upon observable experience or empirical evidence.
- Research is directed towards finding answers to pertinent questions and solutions to problems.
- It emphasizes the development of generalization, principles or theories.
- The purpose of research is not to arrive at an answer, which is personally pleasing to the researcher, but rather one, which will stand up the test of criticism.

Best and Kahn bring out the following attributes or characteristics of research.

i) Research is directed toward the solution of a problem. The ultimate goal is to discover cause and effect relationships between variables.

ii) Research emphasizes the development of gneralisation, principles or theories that will be helpful in predicting future occurrence.

iii) Research is based on observable experience or empirical evidence.

iv) Research demands accurate observation and description.

v) Research involves gathering new data from primary or first hand sources or using existing data for a new purpose.

vi) Research is often characterized by carefully designed procedures that apply rigorous analysis.

vii) Research requires expertise.

viii) Research strives to be objective and logical, applying every possible test to validate the procedures employed, the data collected and the conclusions reached. The researcher attempts to eliminate personal bias.

ix) Research involves the quest for answers to unsolved problems.

x) Research is characterized by patient and unhurried activity. It is rarely spectacular.

xi) Research is carefully recorded and reported.

xii) Research sometimes requires courage. Many important discoveries were made in the history of science in spite of the opposition of political and religious authorities.

PURPOSES OR OBJECTIVES OF RESEARCH

The purpose of research is to discover answers to questions through the application of scientific procedures. These activities pave ways for the development of nascent knowledge and development of knowledge infrastructure and knowledge reservoir for societal development. Each research study has its own specific purpose. According to C.S Kothari the purposes or objectives of research may be grouped under the following heads.

i) To gain familiarity with phenomenon or to achieve new insights into it;

ii) To portray accurately the characteristics of a particular individual, situation or a group ;

iii) To determine the frequency with which something occurs or with which it is associated with something else;

iv) To test a hypothesis of a casual relationship between variables.

Krishnaswami and Ranganatham bring out the varied

objectives or purposes of research as:

* Research extends knowledge of human beings, social life and environment.
* Research unravels the mysteries of nature ; brings to light hidden information that might never be discovered fully during the ordinary course of life.
* Research establishes generalizations and general laws and contributes to theory building in various fields of knowledge.
* Research verifies and tests existing facts and theory and these help improving our knowledge and ability to handle situations and events.
* General laws developed through research may enable us to make reliable predictions of events yet to happen.
* Research aims to analyse interrelationships between variables and derive causal explanations.
* Applied research aims at finding solutions to problems.
* Research also aims at developing new tools, concepts and theories for a better study of unknown phenomenon.
* Research aids planning and thus contributes to national development.

Significance or Uses of Research

Research is a highly intellectual activity. Research findings can become invalid with new advances in knowledge Growth of knowledge is continuum. According to Clifford Hawkins and Marco Sorgi in their book, 'Research' has listed the following benefits or significance of research

i) A critical or scientific attitude is developed;.

ii) Research gives the chance to study a subject in depth;

iii) A researcher knows how to use a library and resources available in different libraries;

iv) A researcher learns to critically assess the literature in the subject of study;

v) Research helps to develop special interests and skills in the researcher;

vi) Helps in understanding the attitude of others whether in routine interactions or research laboratories; and

vii) After successfully completing a research project, a candidate secures a higher degree say M.Phil or Ph.D. Higher qualifications which help the candidate to get promotions to higher posts and higher status in the society.

CHARACTERISTICS OF CONTEMPORARY RESEARCH

The present day research is characterized by the following peculiarities.

Modern research is becoming more and more multidisciplinary in character. The boundaries of discipline-wise research have gone today. New subjects are developing due to the various methods of formation of new subjects such as fusion, agglomeration, partial comprehension, distillation etc. Hence the researchers started in pursuing their research in such subject areas that are multidisciplinary in character.

Professionalism in research is another characteristic of modern research. A profession is an occupation, vocation or career where specialized knowledge of a subject field or science is applied. It is usually applied to occupations that involve prolonged academic training and a formal qualification. It is axiomatic that professional activity involves systematic knowledge and proficiency. Like other professionals like teachers, lawyers, doctors, engineers, librarians, nurses etc the researchers have also become a category in the professional group. Quite a good number of researchers under various categories like research assistants, research associates, research officers are working as professionals in various R & D institutions.

University research has become one of the most important functions in universities in India today. Increase in the number of universities made increase in the research output. Research at doctoral, postdoctoral and project level researches are on the increase. The quantum of research output from universities is considerably significant when compared to research out put from R & D institutions in India.

Funded research has become another characteristic of contemporary research. A number of organizations at national and international level are provided with financial assistance to various institutions to undertake research activities. Organisations such as UGC,AICTE, ICSSR, ICHR, Human Resource Development, CSIR,ICAR, ICMR, DBT etc are some of the important national level organizations. Ford Foundation, UNESCO, UNIDO, FAO of UN system, WHO etc are some of the international agencies providing financial assistance for executing various levels of research work.

Quite a good number of organizations are presently engaged in collaborative and team research. This type of research approach will enable mutual benefits to the participating institutions and qualitative improvement in research.

Research quality assessment measures such as citation analysis has been used today for the evaluation of research performance. Among other outcomes, this has led to the study of rankings of journals, university departments, research institutions and individual scholars and scientists.

When used to study research performance, all publications or a sample, covering a given time period are selected. Research papers published in primary sources are used as units of analysis. Citations to these documents are collected from citation indexes to be analysed to discover the most cited authors or articles and the antecedents or core documents in a given field or discipline. This type of assessment is used for award for meritorious work or even as promotional criteria for assessing researchers' performance.

ICT applications in research, availability of high-tech libraries and information centres, national and international information systems and services in various subjects etc paved the way for quality research. The present avenues of ICT help the researchers to undertake effective and efficient research activities. It may be presumed that globalization would discourage repetitive research and encourage research workers to become more participative and collaborative with their peers working elsewhere. The application of ICT will help in the selection of the relevant topics, avoid duplication of research and avoid spending of unnecessary time for literature survey. This facilitates data analysis and presentation and dissemination of research output speedily and effectively. In fact the application of ICT in modern research has immense benefits in quality research.

The present day ICT applications enable speedier dissemination of research output generated by researchers in various R& D institutions, universities etc. through various types of communication media. This will enable the researchers to avoid repetitive research and to imbue relay research.

TYPES OF RESEARCH

Research can be classified from three perspectives viz i) application of research study; ii) Objectives in undertaking the research; iii) Inquiry mode employed.

The types of research on the basis of application of research study are: i)Basic research; and ii) Applied research.

Basic research or theoretical research or pure research or fundamental research includes studies conducted to achieve a fuller understanding of a phenomenon without consideration of how findings will be applied. Basic research is derived from fundamental, intellectual problems; it tends to be of an original and theoretical nature. A study undertaken primarily to acquire knowledge for its own sake can be classified as basic research. The major objective of basic research lies in designing the tools of analysis and in discovering universal laws and theories. It involves developing and testing theories and hypotheses that are intellectually challenging to the researcher but may not have practical application at the present time or in the future. The developments of various sciences owes much to pure research. The findings of pure research enrich the storehouse of knowledge that can be drawn upon in the future to formulate significant practical researches. Dixey stated that 'natural knowledge pursued for its own sake without any direct view to future utility will often lead to results of most unexpected kind and of very highest practical importance.' General theory of library classification, Five Laws of Library Science of Dr.S.R Ranganathan etc can be considered as examples of basic research in Library Science. Maslow's theories in Management, Newton's Law of motion, Theory of relativity, Theory of origin of species etc can be considered as outcome of basic research.

Applied research or Action research aims at finding a solution for an immediate problem facing a society or an industrial or business organization. In fact, applied research is pragmatic and its purpose is more specific and is generally aimed at solving practical problems. Findings from basic research can be applied for later action research for the solution of practical problems, and data from applied research studies might, in turn, be incorporated into the body of knowledge from which the theoretical problems of basic research are derived. An investigation into catalogue use study in a university library, Information use, use behaviour and use pattern of scientists in special libraries, Investigation into Scientific productivity of agricultural scientists etc can be considered as examples of research topics in the area of applied research.

The distinction between pure and applied research is not absolute, but at best only relative, for pure research may have significant potential for its application to the solution of a practical problem. Goode and Hatt have stated the mutual contribution between pure and applied research as: By developing principle, pure research offers solutions to many practical problems; pure research helps to find the critical factors in a practical problem; pure research develops many alternative solutions and thus enables us to choose the best solution. While in the case of applied research the contributions are: applied research can contribute new facts; applied research can put theory to the test.; applied research may aid in conceptual clarification.

From the viewpoint of objectives, a research can be classified as follows :

Descriptive Research: This attempts to describe systematically a situation, problem, phenomenon, service or programme or provides information about, say living condition of a community, information services in special libraries etc

Co relational Research : It attempts to discover or establish the existence of a relationship or interdependence between two or more aspects of a situation.

Explanatory Research : It attempts to clarify why and how there is a relationship between two or more aspects of a situation or phenomenon.

Exploratory Research: It is undertaken to explore an area where little is known or to investigate the possibilities of undertaking a particular research study.

From the inquiry mode of the process adopted to answer to research questions there are two approaches viz Structured approach and unstructured approach. The structured approach to inquiry is usually classified as quantitative research while unstructured approach is usually classified as qualitative research.

RESEARCH APPROACHES

Research approaches are research methodologies or philosophical approaches to research. They are :

- Descriptive research
- Comparative research
- Exploratory research
- Diagnostic research
- Experimental research; and
- Historical research.

Descriptive research is a sort of survey research at a given time to study, understand and report the present status of a situation. In comparative research it is a type of research describing two or more entities of the same nature, which are compared and contrasted in terms of certain predefined parameters. In the case of exploratory research which explores an area where little is known or investigate the possibilities of undertaking a particular research study. Diagnostic research is a fact-finding aspect of clinical practice. It represents the most typical and simple problem solving strategy. In the case of experimental method it connotes laboratory situation. It is one of the basic methods of research in the field of physical science. Historical research is a method of research into the past of a subject or event, through the study of documentary sources.

REFERENCES

1. Best, John W and Kahn, James V(1986). Research in education. Ed.5. New Delhi, Prentice Hall.
2. Good, V Carter(1959). Introduction to educational research. New Delhi, Prentice -Hall
3. Ghosh, BN(1984) Scientific method and social research. Delhi, Sterling.
4. Kerlinger, Fred W(1973) Foundations of behavioral research. New York, Holt Rinehart and Winston.
5. Khanna, JK and Khurana, S (2007) Handbook of research methodology. Agra, Y.K Publishers.
6. Krishan Kumar (1999)Research methods in Library and Information Science. New Delhi, Har Anand Publicaitons.
7. Krishnaswami, OR and Ranganatham,M(1983)Methodology of research in social sciences. Mumbai,Himalaya Publishing House.
8. Thakur, Devendra (1988). Research methodology in social sciences. New Delhi, Deep and Deep publications.
9. The Encyclopedia of Social Science.V.9. New York, The Macmillan Co.
10. Trochim, William M (2003). Research methods.New Delhi, Biztantra.
11. Young, Pauline V (1977). Scientific social surveys and research. New Delhi, Prentice-Hall.

2

Scientific Method of Research

INTRODUCTION

Scientific method is the pursuit of truth as determined by logical considerations. The ideals of science are to achieve a systematic interrelation of facts. Scientific method refers to a body of techniques for investigating phenomena, acquiring new knowledge, or correcting and integrating previous knowledge. To be termed scientific, a method of inquiry must be based on gathering observable, empirical and measurable evidence subject to specific principles of reasoning. It consists of the collection of data through observation and experimentation and the formulation and testing of hypotheses.

According to Ostele and Mensing scientific method attempts to achieve this ideal by experimentation, observation, logical arguments from accepted postulates and a combination of these three in varying proportions. According to Clover and Balsley 'the scientific method is a systematic step-by-step procedure following the logical processes of reasoning. In fact scientific method is a means for gaining knowledge of the universe.

In the words of Karl Pearson" Scientific method is one and the same in all branches of science and that method is the method of logically trained minds ..... the unity of all sciences consists alone in their methods, not in their materials; the man who classifies facts of any kind whatever, who sees their mutual relation describes their sequences, in applying the scientific method and is a man of science"

Scientific method is an important method of research. It collects facts as historical and descriptive methods do; it interprets and analyses facts as descriptive methods do. In addition, it also tests and verifies data and conclusion either by direct observation or experimentation, and does not accept it unless it is proved by all evidences. Gopal has rightly defined science and scientific method as "the search for truth on the basis of facts and for generalization through a process of induction, deduction, verification, non-suppression of evidence, and open mind" The scientific method does not refer to a field of specific subject of matter, but rather to a procedure or mode of investigation. It is an objective, logical and systematic method of analysis of phenomena, devised to permit the accumulation of reliable knowledge.

ELEMENTS OF SCIENTIFIC METHOD

The elements of scientific method consist of

i) Characterisation (observation and description of phenomena);

ii) Hypothesis development ;

iii) Predictions from the hypothesis;

iv) Experiments ;

v) Evaluation and improvement ; and

vi) confirmation.

Carlos L Lastrucci opines that the scientific method is based on certain basic principles as stated below.

- It relies on empirical evidence;
- It utlilises relevant concepts;
- It is committed to only objective considerations;
- It presupposes ethical neutrality, i.e, it aims at nothing but making only adequate and correct statements about population objects;
- It results into probabilistic predictions;
- Its methodology is made known to all concerned for critical scrutiny and is for use in testing the conclusions through replication ;and
- It aims at formulating most general axioms or what can be termed as scientific theories.

REQUISITES OF A GOOD SCIENTIFIC METHOD

The essentials of a good scientific method stated by the Advisory Committee on Economic and Social Research are:

i) Careful logical analysis of the problem, separating its elements and whenever possible, formulating hypothesis;

ii) Unequivocal definition of terms and concepts and statistical units and measures, so that others will understand exactly and be able to repeat the analysis and test the generalisations;

iii) Collection of data pertinent to the problem under study;

iv) Classification of data;

v) Expression of variables in quantitative terms whenever possible;

vi) Rigorous and exacting experimental or statistical procedure in summarizing the data and in isolating the attributes or variables and measuring their relationship and inter-effects;

vii) Sound logical reasoning as to the testing of hypothesis and drawing generalisations;

viii) Statement of unassailable terms of the exact conclusion arrived at from the findings;

ix) Specific and clear statement of generalizations to facilitate checking and testing by others;

x) Complete elimination of personal equation; and

xi) Complete and careful reporting of the research process, definitions and methods of analysis so that others can check the analysis or test the generalizations with new sets of data.

SCIENTIFIC METHOD OF INQUIRY - PROCESS

A scientific method of inquiry consists of the following processes.

i) State General Problem

Selection of a research problem is an important and premier step in the scientific inquiry. Here the investigator identifies the general area of research. For example user study or catalogue use studies etc can be considered as general areas of research from which specific area can be chosen for a study. The factors like interest of the investigator, significance of the topic etc may be considered as paramount criteria in choosing the area of research.

ii) Conduct Literature Search

A survey of literature in the general area has to be undertaken in this stage. The selection of the specific area of study can often be the byproduct of the extensive survey of literature in the general area. A literature search or literature review is an attempt to identify, locate, synthesise completed research reports, articles, books and other materials about the specific problems of a research topic. The literature search and subsequent review can be of value to researchers by helping them to regard to their studies as contributions to a larger topic of which the inquiry is undertaken.

iii) State Specific Problem

In this stage of the research process, the specific problem to be focused on is identified. The relationship of the question under investigation to the general Research area is also taken into careful consideration, and limitations for the study are identified.. In this stage pertinent independent and dependent variables are identified. So also the problem area under investigation is clearly and precisely outlined.

v) Design Methodology

In this stage of research process the blue print of the procedures and methods relating to the research work is designed. These include population under study, type of sample, operational definitions of the variables, methodologies adopted, data collection methods, data analysis and utilization of statistical techniques.

v) Data Gathering

At this stage of research process, research methods such as interview, questionnaire, observation etc adopted for data collection are to be decided.

vi) Analysis of Data

Data analysis is a research process after data gathering in the field of study. Statistical tools and techniques used in the study are considered in this stage.

vii) Reporting Results

In this stage results of the study are recorded and reported. The report should consist of three elements such as preliminaries, the body and auxiliaries.

viii) Polish and Ramify Hypotheses

The findings of the research study should enable to ramify and test the tenability of the hypotheses formulated in the study.

SPIRAL OF SCIENTIFIC METHOD

Scientific method is characterized by a never ending spiral.

Dr. Ranganathan has conceptualized a spiral of scientific method in order to explain vividly the steps and phases involved in scientific research. The phases in the spiral of scientific method include empirical phase, hypothesizing phase, deductive phase and verification phase, The various phases in the spiral of scientific method is schematically represented in Fig. 1.

The cycle implied in the spiral will be followed in the clock-wise direction. For convenience of study, the four cardinal points of the cycle are denoted by the terms Nadir, Ascendant, Zenith and Descendent. The Nadir marks the accumulation of facts, obtained by observation, experimentation and other forms of experience. The ascendant marks the accumulation of inducted or empirical laws got out of the facts accumulated at the Nadir, by

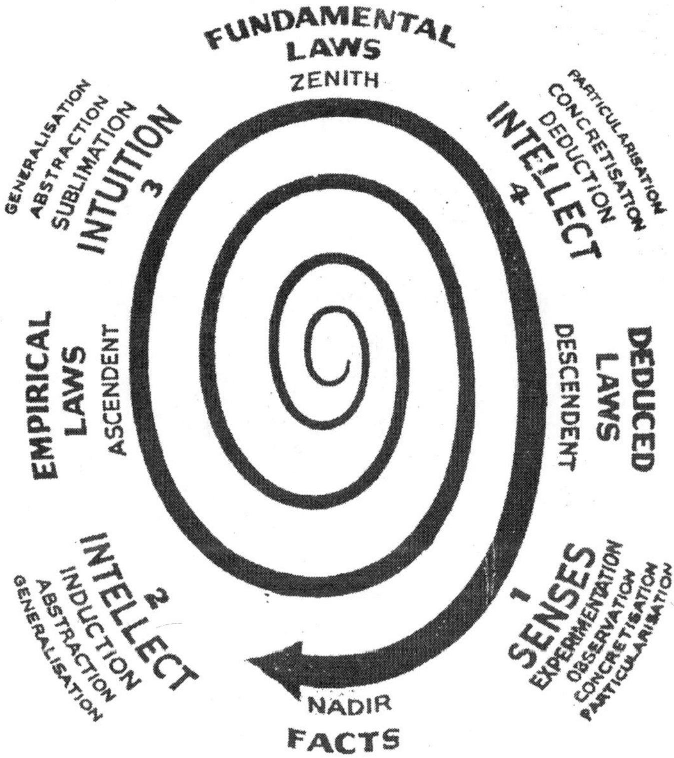

Fig. 1. Spiral of Scientific Method

inductive logic including normal equations and other aids from statistical calculus. The Zenith marks the fundamental laws formulated with the aid of intuition of some degree or other so as to comprehend all the inducted or empirical laws accumulated at the ascendant. The descendent marks the accumulation of the deduced laws got from the fundamental laws at the Zenith, with the aid of deductive logic including general semantics and all kinds of mathematical calculus.

The four cardinal points give rise to four quadrants in the cycle implied in the spiral. For convenience of reference, the Quadrants will be numbered 1 to 4 respectively as follows:

Quadrant 1 is the one between Descendent and Nadir; quadrant 2 is one between Nadir and Ascendant; quadrant 3 is the one between ascendant and zenith; and quadrant 4 is the one between Zenith and Descendent.

The explanations given under state the stages of the universe of knowledge while the spiral travels from quadrant 1 to 4.

Quadrant 1 corresponds to the stage in the development of a domain of the universe of knowledge, conforming to scientific method, in which :

i) Primary senses are used either in their native state or with the aid of instruments of various degrees of powerfulness;

ii) Observations are made of knowees, either with or without experimental interference and conditioning; There is progression towards particularisation, and regression from generalization;

iii) There is progression towards concreteness and, regression from abstractness; and

iv) Facts are found and recorded.

Quadrant 2 corresponds to the stage in which :

i) intellect is used either by itself or aided by machinery constructed to speed up the work of the intellect and to give relief to it in some measure;

ii) reasoning is made with the aid of inductive logic including normal equations and other statistical and other calculuses to boil down the numerous facts accumulated at the Nadir to a small number of inducted or empirical laws;

iii) there is regression from particularization, and progression towards generalization;

v) there is regression from concreteness, and progression towards abstractness; and

vi) inducted or empirical laws are formulated and recorded.

Quadrant 3 corresponds to the stage in which :

i) intuition of some intensity or other is used unmediated by the primary senses or the intellect;

ii) the inducted or empirical laws stand boiled down to a very small number of fundamental laws ;

iii) there is a regression from particularization and progression towards ultimate generalization;

iv) there is a regression from concreteness and progression towards ultimate abstractness; and

v) the fundamental laws are seized and recorded.

Quadrant 4 corresponds to the stage in which :

i) intellect is used either by itself or aided by machinery constructed to speed up the work of the intellect and give relief to it in some measure;

ii) reasoning is made with the aid of deductive logic including general semantics, and mathematical and other calculus to work out all the compelling implications of the fundamental laws;

iii) there is a progression towards particularization, and regression from generalization;

iv) there is progression towards concreteness, and regression from abstractness; and

v) the deducted laws are derived and recorded.

The spiral of scientific method begins the next cycle thereafter, by reentering quadrant 1. Two things happen at the stage of development corresponding to quadrant 1 in the new cycle observations and experiments are made to verify empirically the validity of the new deduced laws and further observations and experiments are made continuously and this leads to accumulation of new empirical facts.

In a study entitled 'Research on universe of subjects, Prof. Neelameghan has underlined the usefulness of spiral of scientific method on the modes of formation of subjects as:

i) It characterizes a discipline on the basis of its method of development rather than on the basis of its subject of study of the method used in studying it;

ii) Any discipline may adopt the scientific method in its development;

iii) Certain specific attributes of the different subjects become clear. This is of help to the librarian in learning about certain affinity among large regions of knowledge such as those comprehended by each basic subject, comprehensive subjects, etc. This is in turn, helps in placing these subjects in a helpful position in the universe of subjects.;

iv) Different models of the development of subjects may be formulated to help the prediction of likely developments in each of the subjects or groups of them; and

v) The facility for the prediction of the trend of development in a subject is valuable to the classificationist and classifier in particular and the librarian in general.

Spiral of scientific method is concerned with verification of the acquired knowledge. It finds out some order in which things are related together. The spiral of scientific method is open-ended in nature, and has unlimited scope for hospitality of various manifestations in any field of knowledge.

REFERENCES

1. Busha, Charles H and Harter,Stephen P(1980) Research methods in Librarianship. New York, Academic Press.
2. Clover, Vernon T and Balsley,Howard L (1979)Business research methods.Ohio, Grid Publishing.
3. Emory, C William(1976). Business research methods. Illinois, Richard D Irwin.Gopal, MH(1970) An introduction to research procedures in social sciences. Bombay, Asia Publishing House.
4. Gosh,BN(1999) Scientific method and social research. New Delhi.
5. Kerlinger, FW(1973).Foundations of behavioural research. New York, Rinehart and Winston.
6. Kothari, CR(2004) Research Methodology :An introduction. New Delhi, New Age
7. Krishan Kumar(1992) Research methods in Library and Information Science. New Delhi, Har-Anand Publications.
8. Krishnaswami,OR and Ranganatham, M(2007) Methodology of research in social sciences. Delhi, Himalaya Pub.House.
9. Neelameghan, A(1976) Resarch on universe of subjects. LSSD.4(1).
10. Pearson, Karl (1911) The grammar of science. London, A and C Black.
11. Ranganathan, SR (1934) Five Laws of Library Science. New Delhi, Asia Pub.
12. Sharma,BAV, et al (1981)Research methods in social sciences. New Delhi, Sterling Publishers.
13. Sharma, Pandy SK(1996) Librarians' knowledge of knowledge. New Delhi, ESS ESS.
14. Young, Pauline V(1977) Scientific social surveys and research. New Delhi, Prentice-Hall of India.

3

Research Problem

INTRODUCTION

The term problem comes from the Greek word Proballein which means anything thrown forward; a question proposed for solution; a matter stated for examination. In the words of R.S Woodworth, a problem is "a situation for which we have no ready and successful response by instinct or by previously acquired habit. We must find out what to do". John Dewey states "the need of clearing up confusion, of straightening out an ambiguity, of overcoming obstacles, of covering the gap between things as they are and as they may be when transformed, is, in germ, a problem" In research process, the first and foremost step is the selection of a research problem. A research problem, in general refers to some difficulty which a researcher experiences in the context of either a theoretical or practical situation and wants to obtain a solution for the same. Solving this difficulty is the task of research.

COMPONENTS OF RESEARCH PROBLEM

The research problem should define the goal of the

researcher in clear terms. It means that along with the problem, the objective of the proposal should adequately be spelled out. The first step in the formulation and specification of a research problem is to make it concrete and explicit. There is no foolproof method by which one can do it.

R.L Ackoff in his book 'The design of social research' provides considerable guidance in identifying and specifying a problem of research. He identifies that a research problem consists of the following components or elements.

Research Consumer : There must be an individual or a group which has some difficulty. The individual may be the researcher himself and the group could be a group of researchers or scientists. For most problems, there are also other participants. The researcher, if he is different from the research-consumer, is participant in the problem. So are all individuals or groups who may be affected by a decision taken by the research-consumer.

Research -Consumer's Objectives: The research consumer must have something he wants to get or some ends he seeks to achieve.

Alternative Means to Achieve the Objectives: The research consumer must have available alternative means for achieving the objectives he desires. Means are courses of action open to the research-consumer. A course of action may involve use of various objects. Objects used thus are the instruments. A scale may be an instrument, but the use of a scale may be conceived of as a means. An instrument refers to any object, concept or idea which can be effectively incorporated in the pursuit of the objective.

Doubt in Regard to Selection of Alternatives: The existence of alternative courses of action is not enough; in order to experience a problem, the research consumer must have some doubt as to which alternative to select. Without such a doubt there can be no problem. The research-consumer must have a question concerning the relative efficiency of the alternative means and he must want to answer it..

There must be one or more Environments to which the difficulty or problem pertains: The change in environment may produce or remove a problem. A research-consumer may have doubts as to which will be the most efficient means in one environment but would have no such doubt in another. Some problems are specific to only one environment while others are quite general.

SOURCES OF RESEARCH PROBLEM

The following sources are helpful to the researchers in identifying research problems.

i) **Business Problems:** A research problem is a felt need, the need may be an answer, or a solution or an improvement in facilities or technology. They may be business policy problems, operational problems, general management problems or functional area problems.

ii) **Day to day problems:** A research problem can be from the day to day experience of the researcher. Every day problems constantly present some thing new and worthy of investigation and it depends on the keenness of observation and sharpness of the intellect of the researcher to knit his daily experience into a research problem.

iii) **Technological Changes:** Technological changes in a fast changing world are constantly bringing forth new problems and thus new opportunities for research.

iv) **Unexplored areas:** Research problems can be both abstract and of applied interest. The researcher may identify the areas in which much work has been done and the areas in which little work has been done or areas in which no work has been done.

v) **Theory of One's Own Interest:** A researcher may also select a problem for investigation from a given theory in which he has considerable interest. In such situations the researcher must have a thorough knowledge of that theory and should be able to explore some unexplained aspects or assumptions of that theory.

vi) **Documentary sources:** Information sources such as subject books, dissertations, theses, articles, state of the art reports, trend reports, research reports, abstracts, seminar and conference proceedings etc are rich in research problems for research investigators.

vii) **Policy Problems:** Government policy measures give rise to both positive and negative impact. The researcher can identify these aspects for the research

viii) **Discussion with Informal Sources:** Non-documentary sources both formal and informal sources such as institutions, learned bodies, information systems, research supervisors, experts in various subjects fields etc are rich in identifying research problems.

ix) Intuition of human mind can also be considered as a source of research problem.

CRITERIA FOR THE SELECTION OF A RESEARCH PROBLEM

The research problem undertaken for study must be carefully selected. The following are some of the guidelines or criteria to be considered by a researcher in the selection of a research problem.

i) The topic selected should be original or at least explored.

ii) It should be of significance and socially relevant and useful

iii) It should be interesting to the researcher and should fit into his aptitude

iv) It should be from the researcher's specialization

v) It should correspond to the researcher's abilities - both acquired and acquirable

vi) It should be good enough to be researchable and small enough to be handled. The topic should be amenable for research with existing and acquirable skills

vii) It should have a clear focus or objective

viii) The feasibility of carrying out research on the selected problem should be checked against the following

- Whether adequate and suitable data are available?
- Whether there is access to the organization and respondents?
- Whether cooperation will be forthcoming from organization and respondents?
- What are the resources required and how are they available?
- Whether the topic is within the resources (money and manpower) position of the researcher?

ix) It should be completed within the time limits permissible.

x) Controversial subject should not become the choice of an average researcher

Goode and Hatt suggest the following criteria for the selection of a research problem

i) The researcher's interest, intellectual curiosity and drive; Practicability;

ii) The urgency of the problem;

iii) Anticipating or expected outcomes. Their importance for the field represented and implementation; and

iv) Resources, training and personal qualifications of the personnel; availability of special equipment, data, methods, time and sponsorship and administrator's cooperation.

Cocharan and Cox suggest that a prospective researcher should put the following questions before the selection of a research problem.

a) Does the field appeal to my interest?

b) Will the results be of practical or utilitarian significance ?

c) Does the field present gaps in verified knowledge which need to be filled?

d) Does the field require working or recasting ?

e) Does the field permit extension of inquiry beyond the present limits or verified knowledge ?

f) Is the field pivotal or strategical from the standpoint of immediate purposes which the results of the proposed investigation are to fulfill ?

The selection or choice of a research problem is a difficult job in spite of the guidelines or criteria put forward by various schools of thought. The guidelines suggested above, study of literature in the field of study and related topics and discussion with experts in the field would immensely help the researcher in the selection of a research problem.

FACTORS AFFECTING THE CHOICE IN THE RESEARCH PROBLEM

A number of factors influence the ultimate selection of the research problem. The important factors are:

i) Sociological paradigm - a model or school of thought with which the researcher identifies ; there are a number of distinct paradigms within social science, and most of these differ in values, methodology, degree of reactivity involved, scope and time;

ii) The researcher's values - values affect not only the problem deemed worthy of research but also the method considered appropriate and the way the researcher views the relationship between him or herself and his or her subjects;

iii) The degree of reactivity inherent in the particular method deemed appropriate for gathering data on the research problem that is chosen-the study can affect the data, as when the group being observed acts one way in the presence of an observer and differently when the observer is not present;

iv) The researcher's methodology, including the degree of proof he or she requires in order to consider the hypothesis proven ;

v) The unit of analysis chosen - whether the unit of analysis is small, such an individual person or large such as a country; and

vi) The time factor - whether the study deals with a cross section of the population at one point in time or is a longitudinal study conducted over time.

DEFINING THE RESEARCH PROBLEM

Defining a research problem is the fuel that drives the scientific process, and is the foundation of any research method and experimental design, from true experiment to case study. The problem to be investigated must be defined unambiguously for that will help to distinguish relevant data from the irrelevant ones. A proper definition of research problem will enable the researcher to be on the track whereas an ill-defined problem may create hurdles. Defining a research problem properly is a prerequisite for any study and is a step of the highest importance. In fact, formulation of a problem is often more essential than its solution. It is only careful detailing the research problem so that we can work out the research design and can smoothly carry on all the conceptual steps while doing research. In other words, defining a problem involves the task of laying down boundaries within which a researcher shall study the problem with a pre-determined objective in view.

The technique involved in the defining of a research problem is a systematic one which comprises the following steps in order.

Statement of the Problem in a General Way

In this step the problem should be stated in a broad general way, keeping in view either some practical concern or some scientific or intellectual interest. For this purpose, the researcher must immerse himself thoroughly in the subject matter concerning which he wishes to pose a problem. It is considered advisable to do some field observation and for that purpose the researcher may undertake some sort of preliminary survey or pilot survey. The problem stated in a broad general way may contain various ambiguities which must be resolved by thinking and rethinking over the problem. At the same time the feasibility of a particular solution has to be considered and the same should be kept in view while stating the problem.

Understanding the Nature of the Problem.

The second step in defining the problem is to understand its origin and nature clearly. The best way of understanding the problem is to discuss it with those who first raised it in order to find out how the problem originally came about and with what objectives in view. For a better understanding of the nature of the problem involved, he can enter into discussion with those who have good knowledge of the problem concerned or similar other problems.

Surveying the Available Literature

A survey of literature concerning the problem at hand must necessarily be examined before a definition of the research problem is given. This means that the researcher must be well-conversant with relevant theories in the field, reports and records as also all other relevant literature. The researcher must devote sufficient time in reviewing research already undertaken on related problems. Studies on related problems are useful for indicating the type of difficulties that may be encountered in the present study as also the possible analytical shortcomings. At times such studies may also suggest useful and even new lines of approach to the present problem.

Developing the Ideas through Discussions

Discussion concerning a problem often produces useful information or new ideas. Hence, a researcher must discuss his research problem with his colleagues and others who are rich in experience in the field of study. This type of experience survey would help the researcher to sharpen his focus of attention on the topic under consideration.

Rephrasing the Research Problem

In the final step the researcher must rephrase the research problem into working proposition. Through rephrasing, the researcher puts the research problem in specific terms as possible so that it may become operationally viable and may help in the development of working hypotheses.

Kothari has opined that the following points must be observed while defining a research problem.

a) Technical terms and words or phrases, with special meanings used in the statement of the problem, should be clearly defined.

b) Basic assumptions or postulates relating to the research problem should be clearly stated.

c) A straight forward statement of the value of the investigation (i.e the criteria for the selection of the problem) should be provided.

d) The suitability of the time -period and the sources of data available must also be considered by the researcher in defining the problem.

e) The scope of the investigation or limits within which the problem is to be studied must be mentioned explicitly in defining the research problem.

Formulation of the Objectives of the Study

Having selected and specified the research problem, the next step is to formulate the objectives of research. Research is not for the sake of research. It is undertaken to achieve goals. Thus research is a goal-oriented activity. The researcher has to identify the goal(s) to be achieved and they must be specified in order to give direction to the research study. Once formulation of research objectives is stated, then the entire research activity will be geared to achieving those objectives. For example, the objectives formulated for a research problem, "An investigation into the scientific productivity of faculty members of Kerala Agricultural University" is given below.

The main objective of the study is to examine the scientific productivity of faculty members in agriculture. The specific objectives are :

i) to identify the quantitative assessment of productivity in terms of year-wise and form-wise contribution;

ii) to examine the subject-wise distribution of publications in agricultural science;

iii) to determine the authorship pattern and to find out the extent of author collaboration;

iv) to find out the most productive journals selected by the scientists to publish their articles; and

v) to ascertain the growth pattern of agricultural science literature by calculating relative growth rate.

REFERENCES

1. Ackoff, RL(1953) The design of research. Chicago, University of Chicago Press.

2. Bhandarkar, PL and Wilkinson, TS(2010) Methodology and techniques of social research. Mumbai, Himalaya Pub.House.

3. Busha, Charles H and Harter. S P(1980) Research methods in librarianship. New York, Academic Press.

4. Khanna, JK and Khurana, S(2007) Handbook of research methodology.Agra, Y.K.Publishers.

5. Kothari, CR(2004) Research methodology, methods and techniques. New Delhi, New Age.

4

Hypotheses

INTRODUCTION

The derivation of a suitable hypothesis goes hand in hand with the selection of a research problem. A hypothesis is a conjectural statement of the relation between two or more variables. It is desirable that the researcher should propose a set of suggested solutions or explanations of the difficulty which the research proposes to solve. Such tentative solutions formulated as a proposition are called, hypothesis for which imaginative data may not be the real solutions to the problem.

MEANING OF HYPOTHESIS

The word hypothesis is a combination of two terms, hypo and thesis. The meaning of hypo is less than. So the meaning of the word hypothesis is less than a thesis. Hypothesis is a statement, temporally accepted as true in the light of what it is, at the time, known about a phenomenon, and it is employed as a basis for action in the search for new truth. It is a tentative assumption drawn from knowledge and theory which is used as a guide in the investigation of other facts and theories that are yet unknown.

Webster's New International Dictionary of English Language defines the term 'hypothesis' as 'proposition, condition or principle which is assumed, perhaps without belief, in order to draw out its logical consequences and by this method to test its accord with facts which are known or may be determined'

G.A Lundberg defines, " a hypothesis is a tentative generalization, the validity of which remains to be tested. In the most elementary stage the hypothesis may be any guess, hunch, imaginative idea, which becomes the basis for action or investigation". In the words of Goode and Hatt "It is a proposition which can be put to test to determine validity". Rummel and Ballaine defines that "A hypothesis is a question put in such a way that an answer of some kind can be forth coming" According to Werkmeister, 'the guesses he(Scientist) makes are the hypotheses which either solve the problems or guide him in further investigation'

The analytical approach to the above definitions leads us to conclude that a hypothesis is a tentative solution or explanation or a guess or assumption or a proposition or a statement of the problem facing the researcher, adopted on a cursory observation of known and available data, as a basis of investigation, whose validity is to be tested or verified.

ROLE OF HYPOTHESIS IN RESEARCH

Hypothesis has a very important place in research. It is almost impossible for a research worker, not to have one or more hypothesis before processing with his work. The importance/role of hypothesis in research can be stated as under:

a) Hypothesis provides direction to the research. It defines which is relevant and what is irrelevant. Thus it prevents the review of irrelevant literature and the collection of useless or excess data. It also ensures the collection of data necessary to answer the question posed in the statement of the problem.

b) It sensitizes the investigator to certain aspects of the situation which are relevant from the standpoint of the problem at hand.

c) It is a guide to the thinking process and the process of discovery.

d) It focuses on research, without hypothesis research would be like a random and aimless wandering.

e) It prevents blind research. It also prevents indiscriminate gathering of data which may later turn out to be irrelevant.

f) It sensitizes the individual facts and conditions that might otherwise be overlooked

g) Hypothesis places clear and specific goals before us. These clear and specific goals provide the investigator with a basis for selecting samples and research procedures to meet the following goals

    i) It serves the function of lining together related facts and information and organizing them into one comprehensible whole.

    ii) It enables the investigator to understand with greater clarity his problem and its ramifications, as well as the data which bear on it

    iii) It further enables a researcher to clarify the procedures and methods to be used in solving his problem and to rule out methods which are incapable of providing the necessary data.

iv) It serves as a framework for drawing conclusions. It makes possible the interpretation of data in the light of tentative proposition or provisional guess. It provides the outline for stating conclusions in a meaningful way.

TYPES OF HYPOTHESES

Hypotheses can be classified in a variety of ways. Classification of hypotheses on the basis of their levels of abstraction is considered as a fruitful one. Goode and Hatt have identified three differential levels of abstraction reached by hypotheses. The levels are :

i) At the lowest level of abstraction are the hypotheses which state existence of certain empirical uniformities. Many types of such empirical uniformities are common in social research. The hypothesis of this type frequently seems to invite scientific verification of what are called 'common sense propositions' indeed without much justification.

ii) At a relatively higher level of abstraction are hypotheses concerned with complex 'ideal types'. These hypotheses aim at testing whether logically derived relationship between empirical uniformities obtains. This level of hypothesizing moves beyond the level of anticipating a simple empirical uniformity by visualising a complex referent in society.

iii) Hypotheses at the highest level of abstraction are category of hypotheses concerned with the relation obtaining amongst analytic variables. Such hypotheses are statements about how one property affects other e.g Impact of information technology on education or deforestation and soil erosion.

Another classification of hypotheses is given under.

a) **Explanatory Hypothesis:** The purpose of this hypothesis is to explain a certain fact. All hypotheses are in a way explanatory for a hypothesis is advanced only when we try to explain the observed fact.. A large number of hypotheses are advanced to explain the individual facts in life.

b) **Descriptive Hypothesis:** Some times a researcher comes across a complex phenomenon. A hypothesis is descriptive when it is based upon the points of resemblance of some thing. It describes the cause and effect relationship of a phenomenon

c) **Analogical Hypothesis:** When we formulate a hypothesis on the basis of similarities or analogies, it is called an analogical hypothesis

d) **Working Hypothesis:** Some times certain facts cannot be explained adequately by existing hypotheses, and no new hypothesis may come up. Thus, the investigation may be held up. In this situation, a researcher formulates a hypothesis which enables to continue investigation. Such a hypothesis formulated for the purpose of further investigation is called working hypothesis.

e) **Null Hypothesis:** In the early stages of the study, researchers state an affirmative scientific or research hypothesis as a prediction of the outcome that they propose to test. Later, at the stage of the statistical analysis of the observed data, they restate the hypothesis in negative or null form. The null hypothesis relates to a statistical method of interpreting conclusions about population characteristics that are inferred from the variable relationships observed in samples. Most hypotheses are the opposite of the null hypothesis.

SOURCES OF HYPOTHESIS

The derivation of a good hypothesis demands characteristics of experience and creativity. Some degree of data gathering, the review of related literature, or a pilot study must precede the development and gradual refinement of the hypothesis. A good investigator must have not only an alert mind capable of deriving relevant hypothesis, but also a critical mind capable of rejecting faulty hypotheses. The specific sources of hypotheses are:

i) **General Culture:** In the investigations for solving problems of Indian education our hypotheses cannot lose sight of the broad general culture to which we belong. While formulating such hypotheses we cannot ignore religious or moral bias in Indian education, typical role of family in Indian education, play interests of Indian children, our prejudices against women education, compulsory education or co-education. Our cultural heritage is a great source of ideas, theories, tentative theories and provisional propositions.

ii) **Personal Experience:** Some of our personal experiences may be directly changed into research hypothesis, for example Teacher's character and personality are imbibed by the students, good study habits improve achievement, library reading enhances interest in knowledge etc.

iii) **Scientific Theory:** There are various scientific laws or theories which are transferable to the field of educational researches. For example, we have theories like sound mind in a sound body, handicapped children face adjustment problems etc

iv) **Analogies:** Although reasoning analogy generally is considered unacceptable as a source of proof, it is a very rich source of hypothesis It is the process of framing hypothesis from the likeness and similarities. It is assumed that the existence of similarities between two situations is not accidental, but that it is the result of the operation of some law common to the situations.

CHARACTERISTICS OF HYPOTHESIS

The significant characteristics and features of hypothesis are the following

a) A good hypothesis is in agreement with the observed facts.

A single unexplained conflict between fact and hypothesis is disastrous to the latter. A hypothesis must be entirely plausible and conceivable. It should be based directly on the existing data.

b) A good hypothesis does not conflict with any law of nature which is known to be true.

There are a number of conflicting theories of learning and teaching. These conflicts arise partly out of the failure of research workers to produce hypothesis that are in agreement with fact and are not in conflict with any law of nature.

c) Good hypothesis is Expert.

It is stated in a scientific and research like language and is not an ordinary statement.

d) A good hypothesis is stated in the simplest possible terms.

It is also called the principle of economy. The number of hypotheses must also not be needlessly multiplied.

e) A good hypothesis permits the application of deductive reasoning.

It should be verifiable and testable. A hypothesis cannot be verified until deductions can be made from it which are capable of empirical verifications.

f) It should be so designed that its test will provide an answer to the original problem which forms the primary purpose of the investigation.

g) It must be stated in final form early in the experiment before any attempt at verification is made.

CRITERIA FOR WORKABLE HYPOTHESIS

The formal conditions laid down by thinkers provide the criteria for judging a hypothesis as good or valid. These criteria are as follows:

i) A hypothesis should be empirically verifiable

ii) A hypothesis should be relevant

iii) A hypothesis must have predictive and explanatory power

iv) A hypothesis must furnish a base for deductive inference on consequences

v) A hypothesis should not go against the traditionally established knowledge

vi) A hypothesis should be simple

vii) A hypothesis must be clear, definite and certain

viii) Hypothesis should be related to available techniques.

STAGES IN THE FORMULATION OF HYPOTHESIS

There are four stages in the development of hypothesis. The first stage is feeling of a problem. The observation and analysis of the researcher reveals certain facts. These facts pose a problem. The second stage is formulation of a hypothesis or hypotheses. A tentative supposition/guess is made to explain the facts which call for an explanation. At this stage some past experience is necessary to pick up the significant aspects of the observed facts. The third stage is deductive development of hypothesis using deductive reasoning. The last stage is the verification or testing of hypothesis. This consists in finding whether the hypothesis agrees with the facts. If the hypothesis stands the test of verification, it is accepted as an explanation of the problem. If it does not agree it is said to be false. Such a false hypothesis is either totally rejected or modified. Verification hypothesis is of two types viz direct verification and indirect verification.

TESTING OF HYPOTHESIS

Testing of hypothesis is done directly or indirectly through logical methods. Testing of the hypothesis is also carried out by using statistical methods. Testing is used to accept or reject an assumption or hypothesis about a random variable using a sample from the distribution. Statistical tests such as t-test, Z-test can be used to find out the tenability of the hypothesis.

USES OF HYPOTHESIS IN RESEARCH

The uses or advantages of hypothesis are the following

i) It is a starting point for many a research work.

ii) It helps in deciding the direction in which to proceed.

iii) It helps in selecting and collecting pertinent facts.

iv) It is an aid to explanation.

v) It helps in drawing specific conclusions

vi) It helps in testing theories.

vii) It works as a basis for future knowledge.

REFERENCES

1. Bhandarkar, PL and Wilkinson, TS(2010) Methodology and techniques of social research.New Delhi, Himalaya Pub. House.

2. Goode and Hatt Khanna, JK and Khurana, S(2007) Handbook of research methodology. Agra, YK publishers.

3. Kothari, CR Krishnaswami, OR and Ranganatham, M(2005) Methodology of research in social sciences. Delhi, Himalya publishing House.

4. Webster's New International Dictionary of English Language

5. Werkmeister,WH(1948)Basisand structure of knowledge. New York, Harper and Bros.

5

Areas of Research in Library and Information Science

INTRODUCTION

The subject 'Library and Information science does not claim a long tradition of organized research or scholarship. It was initiated only in the first half of the 20th century. The research activities include research conducted in library schools leading to the award of research degree or fellowship by professional associations or research institutions and research was carried out by individual researcher or research teams in library schools, libraries, documentation centres etc in order to solve certain problems that they met in their course of work.

In the field of library science research USA made the premier attempt. Organised research in Library Science was started in USA at the Graduate Library school at the University of Chicago in 1928 with a grant of one million dollar from the Carnegie corporation for advanced research in Library science. The study entitled ' A guide to sources of seventeenth century English history in selected reports of the Royal commission on historical manuscripts' by Eleanor S Upton was awarded Ph.D by the Chicago university in 1930 and is considered as the first doctoral degree in Library science. The study by Rolland E Steven viz, 'The use of library materials in doctoral research' was awarded Ph.D in Library Science by the University of Illinois in 1951.

During 1950s universities viz Illinois, Michigan, Columbia, Western Reserve, California and Rutgers produced 129 Ph.D dissertations. The analysis of areas selected for the research include: 45 studies dealing with history of books, printing, publishing and the history of individual libraries; 13 studies on library governance and administration ; 11 studies on technical services; 9 studies on reading and reading interests; 8 studies on content analysis; 9 studies on bibliographic organisation. Library schools in USA focused their research during 1990s in the following areas.

I. Management: collection development, personal administration, public information services and technical services in different types of libraries.

II. Utilization of variety of communication media and technologies in library and information centres.

III. Acquisition and processing of different types of documents.

IV. Information systems, documentation, information technology, information storage and data processing in libraries and information centres.

V. User studies

VI. Library and Information science education

VII. Micrographics: Their production, storage and organization

VIII. Databases: Generation, management and services.

The present trend in research in Library and information science include globalization and information technologies; social studies and finance and personal investing; social studies of mobile communication; history of libraries; information science and knowledge management ; social history of telecommunications and information infrastructures; the political economy of global information; policy and strategic issues in electronic scholarly publishing.

Research in Library science in UK was started during 1930s. The first doctoral thesis accepted by the London School of Economics was on a core library science subject in 1935. The title of the thesis was ' The public library service under English local government'. The areas of research selected by library schools include novel methods of representing and storing of data; Chemical structure of information for manipulation and retrieval; user studies; systems evaluation; organizational problems in the application of information technology; technology transfer and policies; information systems in developing countries; education and training of information specialists; computer-based aids for on-line education; public library services; community information; computer in libraries; expert systems; use of automatic classification; classification techniques for document retrieval; application of parallel processing techniques to information retrieval etc.

Research topics discussed at the Library Theory and Research Sections to the last eight IFLA conferences could be seen as indicative of the work underway worldwide. They cover a wide range : teaching research methods, Library and Information Science research for social development, bibliometrics, digital libraries, professional communications, LIS research in Asia and EU, library history, ZLIS research itself, codes of ethics, multicultural library service provision and collaboration between theory and practice. Research into issues of scholarly communication and the sub-issues of copyright and publication licensing have occupied the more practical research projects of large research libraries around the world. The public library's role in society has underpinned the research in that area.

Research in Library science in India was initiated by Dr. S.R Ranganathan in 1951. The first Ph.D in Library science was awarded to Dr.D.B Krisha Rao for his study on 'Facet analysis and depth classification of agriculture' under the guidance of Dr.S.R Ranganathan and S.Dasgupta. The second Ph.D in Library science was awarded to PSK Sharma for his study on DDC scheme for Indology under the guidance of Dr. JS Sharma in 1977. The subject areas undertaken in Library and Information science research include; Library management ; technical organization ; indexing languages; Use of communication media; user studies, application of computers in library and information field,; use of Information technology in libraries; bibliometrics and scientometics studies; user education and information literacy etc.

A study conducted by Varalekshmi on research areas and trends in library and information science in India pointed out the following.

i) The doctoral research after Dr.S.R Ranganathan has contributed in a limited way to the theoretical base of the subject as majority of the works were on applied aspects. There was no effort to generate knowledge to build a sound body of theory. This has led to a situation of stagnation of knowledgebase. However, a few contributions in classification, cataloguing and information technologies have brightened the otherwise gloomy picture.

ii) Majority of research programmes have described the

existing status of library and information system. In other words, the research depends exclusively on the knowledge of actual experience and not on creativity, probing innovation etc. Moreover, it is far from clear whether the profession at large has taken any advantage of these research findings.

iii) Some of the research topics selected are trivial and non challenging. This diminishes the quality of research.

iv) There is a shortage of investigation in subject areas such as information storage and retrieval, methods to increase resource sharing, scientific communication and its channelisation, education for library and information science.

REFERENCES

1. Ackoff, RL(1961) The design of Social Research.Chicago, Chicago Univ.Press.

2. Busha, Charles H and Harter, Stephen P(1980) Research methods in librarianship. New York, Academic Press.

3. Devarajan, G(1995) Library science education and manpower. New Delhi, ESS ESS.

4. Gopal Lal Jain(1998) Research Methodology: Methods, Tools and Techniques.Jaipur, Mangal Deep Publications

5. Kothari, CR(2004) Research methodology, Methods and Techniques.New Delhi, New Age.

6. Mangla, PB,Ed(1981) Library and Information Science education in India. Delhi, Macmillan.

7. Varaleksmy, RSR(1994) Library and Information Science research in India: subject perspectives. Library Science.31(2).

6

Data Collection and Sampling

TYPES OF DATA

The collective recording of information, either numerical or otherwise is called data. Considering the measurability characteristic of data it can be divided into Qualitative data and quantitative data.

Qualitative data is defined as the data that is not preciously measurable. It is subjective measurement and can vary between observers. Since the qualitative data is attributable to some quality, it is also known as attribute. Satisfaction level of users in a library can be considered an example to qualitative data.

Quantitative data is defined as the data which is accurately measurable by some instrument, device or some technique. In this case there may not be any difference in the value between observers. It is also known as numerical data. Number of users in library, number of periodicals in a special library etc can be considered quantitative data or numerical data.

On the basis of nature of the collection procedure, data can be grouped under the following types

- Primary data
- Secondary data
- Tertiary data

Primary data are those which are collected fresh and for the first time, and thus happen to be original in character. It is collected by the investigator himself or by his subordinates directly from the source of information. Primary data is new data used for the first time to answer specific questions or social issues. Data collected through direct personal observation, data collected through questionnaire method, data collected through interview, data collected through experimentation etc can be considered primary data.

Secondary data are those which have already been collected by some one else and which have already been passed through the statistical process . These data are those generated by another researcher either for some general purpose or for a specific research project. The main purpose in data collection of the secondary user may be different from the original data generator. Data available in the census reports, data available in statistical tools etc which may be used for another study may be considered secondary data.

In tertiary data the researcher is two steps away from the original primary data. Published reports of research and officially collected statistics invariably include tables of data that have summarized, categorized or otherwise manipulated raw data.

The researcher would have to decide which sort of data he would be using for his study and accordingly he will have to select one or the other method of data collection. The methods of collecting primary, secondary and tertiary data differ since primary data are to be originally collected , while in the case of secondary data and tertiary data collection work is merely of compilation.

SAMPLING

Sampling may be defined as the selection of some part of an aggregate or totality on the basis of which a judgment or inference about the aggregate or totality is made. In fact, it is the process of obtaining information about an entire population by examining only a part of it. The usual approach happens to be to make generalizations or to draw inferences based on samples about parameters of population from which the sample is taken.

Data collected may be by any of the methods such as census method or sample method. In the census method, data is collected from all elements of the universe or the entire population in the field of study. In the case of sample method data from every units of the universe is not collected. The collected data is the representative units of the universe of population. The characteristic of this method is that the sample should be the representative of the whole population.

NEED FOR SAMPLING

According to Kothari Sampling is used in practice for a variety of reasons. They are:

i) Sampling can save time and money;

ii) Sampling may enable more accurate measurements for a sample study is generally conducted by trained and experienced investigators;

iii) Sampling remains the only way when population

contains infinitely many members;

iv) Sampling remains the only choice when a test involves the destruction of the item under study; and

v) Sampling usually enables to estimate the sampling errors and, thus assist in obtaining information concerning some characteristic of the population.

SAMPLING DESIGN

Sample design is a definite plan for obtaining a sample from a given population. It refers to the technique or the procedure the researcher would adopt in selecting items for the sample. Researchers must prepare a sample design which should be reliable and appropriate for his research study. While developing a sampling design , the researcher must pay attention to the following steps.

- Type of universe
- Sampling units
- Source list
- Size of sample
- Parameters of interest
- Budgetary constraint
- Sampling procedure.

TYPES OF SAMPLE DESIGN

The sample design is broadly divided into two types. They are probability sampling and non- probability sampling.

Probability sampling is also known as random sampling or chance sampling. In this sampling design every item of the universe has an equal chance of inclusion in the sample. It is only blind chance that determines whether one item or the other is selected. Random sampling ensures the law of statistical regularity which states that if in an average the sample chosen is a random one, the sample will have the same composition and characteristic as the universe. This is the reason why random sampling is considered the best technique of selecting a representative sample.

Random sampling design consists of

- Systematic sampling
- Stratified sampling
- Cluster sampling
- Area sampling
- Multi-stage sampling
- Sampling with probability proportional to size
- Sequential sampling
- Snow ball sampling.

Non-probability sampling is that sampling procedure which does not afford any basis for estimating the probability that each item in the population will be included in the sample. It is also known as deliberate sampling, purposive sampling, judgment sampling. In this method of sampling, items for the sample are selected deliberately by the researcher, his choice concerning the items remaining supreme. Quota sampling is an example of non-probability sampling.

REFERENCES

1. Goodman, LA(1961)Snow ball sampling. Annals of mathematical statistics.32.pp.148-170.
2. Kish,Leslie(1965) Survey sampling. New York, John Wiley.

7

Research Methods and Tools

There are a number of methods or techniques available to the researchers for collection of data in the form of primary data, secondary data and tertiary data. A researcher should judiciously select the method /methods for his own study, keeping in view the factors such as : i) Nature, scope and object of inquiry; ii) Time factor; iii) Availability of funds; and iv) precision required. The important data collection methods include i) Literature survey; ii) Questionnaire method; iii) Interview; iv) Observation; v) Experimentation; vi) Case study; vii) Historical method; viii) Delphi technique; viii) Brain storming technique etc.

LITERATURE SURVEY

Literature survey or literature review is a data collection method focused on documentary sources. Busha and Harter define literature survey as an attempt to identify, locate and synthesize completed research reports, articles, books, and other materials about the specific problems of a research topic. The literature search and subsequent review can be of value to researchers by helping them to regard their studies as contributions to a larger topic of which the inquiry at hand is only a part. Other benefits of literature reviews are that they: i) help to narrow and more clearly delineate the research problem ;ii) reveal overlooked conclusions and facts that ought to be taken into consideration before a research project is actually initiated; iii) suggest new approaches to the planning of investigations; iv) uncover methodologies that were used successfully by other research workers; v) help in the determination of the degree to which particular problems have already been investigated; and vi)assist investigators to develop firmer understandings of theoretical implications of proposed inquiries.

Literature search is carried out by examination of documentary sources such as primary, secondary and tertiary sources. The search strategy in the search of literature can be started from tertiary sources since these are the key to open secondary and primary sources. Tertiary sources such as bibliography of bibliographies, guide to literature, state-of -the -art reports, trend reports etc can be consulted to find out secondary sources and primary sources. Secondary sources viz library catalogue, reference books and bibliographies, books, indexing periodicals, abstracting periodicals, reviewing periodicals, etc in the relevant field of study can be consulted as part of literature search.. Secondary periodicals in various subjects such as Library and Information Science Abstract(LISA) in Library and Information Science, Chemical abstract services (CAS) in Chemistry, Biological Abstract(BA) in Biological science, Physics Abstracts in Physics, Psychological Abstracts in Psychology etc are international abstracting periodicals that can be consulted by the researchers in various subjects as part of literature search.

A researcher can consult Specialised bibliographies, national bibliographies, union catalogues etc as sources for data collection.

Bibliographies on theses and dissertations contain sources of information about completed research. Biographical data sources, encyclopedias, etc are also secondary sources for literature search.

The search of tertiary and secondary sources pave ways for the identification of the primary information sources which are the carriers of nascent knowledge in the field of study. Literature search on sources such as periodical articles, research reports, dissertations and theses, patents, standards, trade literature, seminar and conference papers, government publications etc can be carried out by the researcher.

The decision concerning the use of primary, secondary and tertiary sources for the preparation of review depends largely on the nature of research study proposed by the researcher. If it is a study in an area in which much research has been reported, then a review of the primary sources would be a logical first step. On the other hand, if the study is in an area in which little or no research has been conducted, a check of tertiary and secondary sources is more logical. The researcher must, therefore, develop the expertise and strategies to use information sources without much loss of time and energy.

QUESTIONNAIRE METHOD

Questionnaire is widely used for data collection in research especially in social science research. It is a fairly reliable tool for gathering data from large, diverse, varied and scattered social groups It is used in obtaining quantitative data as well as in gathering information of qualitative nature. It is treated as the 'heart of the survey operation'.

Goode and Hatt state that questionnaire is a device for securing answers to questions by using a form which the respondent fills in himself. Bogardus states that it is a list of questions sent to a number of persons for their answers and which obtains standardized results that can be tabulated and treated statistically. The Dictionary of Statistical Terms defines it as a 'group of or sequences of questions designed to elicit information upon a subject or sequence of subjects from an information'. From all these definitions it becomes clear that questionnaire is a set of questions which is sent to respondents and for which the investigator himself does not go to the informant for collecting information. The respondents send reply by filling in the questionnaire and the information is then fed into the research project.

TYPES OF QUESTIONNAIRES

The questionnaire may be broadly divided into:

* Structured Questionnaire; and
* Unstructured Questionnaire.

In the words of Pauline V Young structured questionnaire are those " which pose definite, concrete, and preordained questions, that is, they are prepared in advance and not constructed on the spot during the question period' The unstructured questionnaire contains a set of questions which are not structured in advance and which may be adjusted according to the needs of question period. The unstructured questionnaire is mainly used for conducting interviews.

CHARACTERISTICS OF A GOOD QUESTIONNAIRE.

The important characteristics or attributes of a good questionnaire are:

- It should enthuse the respondent to give response
- It seeks only that data which cannot be obtained from the information sources such as books, reports etc
- It is as short as possible
- It is comprehensive so that it does not leave out any relevant information
- It is attractive in appearance, neatly arranged and printed
- Directions are clear and complete, important terms are clarified, each question deals with a single idea and worded simple and clear
- Questions are presented in a logical order
- Items are arranged in groups to ensure easy and accurate responses
- Descriptive adjectives and adverbs that have no agreed upon meanings are avoided
- Double negatives are avoided
- Questions that hurts the sentimental feelings of the respondent are avoided

DESIGNING OF A QUESTIONNAIRE

In the designing of a questionnaire, due attention should be paid by the investigator keeping in view the aspects stated above. Consultation with experts should also be attempted in the preparation of a questionnaire. After the preparation of the questionnaire it should be subjected to pre-test by getting the questionnaire filled up by a few respondents in the population under study. In the light of pre-test the final form of the questionnaire may be decided. The questionnaire should also be accompanied by a covering letter stating the objective of the study and requesting the whole-hearted cooperation of the respondent.. The name and address of the investigator should also be given therein. The present trend in the survey studies shows that majority of the investigators use the questionnaire method as one of the preferred techniques for data collection This may be due to the simplicity of the method and the convenience in conducting a survey study. If the population is large and geographically dispersed, questionnaire method is more suitable, less expensive when compared to other survey methods. A model questionnaire for conducting a survey is given below.

QESTIONNAIRE

Users' survey in a university Library

(Please put tick mark where box is available and write wherever necessary)

A. General

1. Name.......
2. Designation

   Student ( )

   Research Scholar ( )

   Teachers ( )

   Others ( )
3. Languages known

   English ( )

   Malayalam ( )

Hindi ( )

Others (Specify) ( )

4. Qualifications ....

5. Area of subject interest ....

B. Physical Facilities

1. Do you use the university library regularly

   yes ( )

   No ( )

2. How do you find the general layout of the library ?

   Easy to follow ( )

   Difficult ( )

   Inconvenient ( )

3. When you wish to use the library, do you find a place in the following sections.

   a) Periodical section always ( )

      usually ( )

      sometimes ( )

      never ( )

   b) Reference section

   c) Stack room section

   d) General reading section

   e) Any other section (specify)

4. What is your opinion regarding the physical facilities available in the library?

   Adequate ( )

   Partially adequate ( )

Inadequate ( )

C. Collection

1. To what extent your requirements are fulfilled by the following information sources(put your preference by 1, 2, 3 etc.)

   Adequate ( )

   partially adequate ( )

   inadequate ( )

   i) periodicals

   ii) Books

   iii) Reference books

   iv) Technical reports

   v) Patents

   vi) Seminar proceedings

   vii) Dissertations and theses

   viii) Indexing and abstracting periodicals

   ix) Bibliographies

2. Do you get your reading materials in due time?

   Always ( )

   Sometimes ( )

   Never ( )

3. Do you feel that useful periodicals subscribed earlier in the university library are discontinued?

   Yes ( )

   NO ( )

   If your answer is YES, mention such periodicals which

must be essentially subscribed to by the library in the order of your preference.

1......

2......

3........

4........

4. Do you use non-book materials ?

Yes ( )

No ( )

If your answer is YES, state to what extent your requirements are met by these collections

Adequate ( )

Partially adequate ( )

Inadequate ( )

5. Do you visit other libraries in case your requirements are not fully met by the university library ?

Yes ( )

No ( )

If the answer is YES, please name the libraries

i)

ii)

iii)

D. Staff

1. Have you ever asked for assistance from library staff for the following purposes.

   a) To locate books

yes ( )

No ( )

b) To locate current and back volumes of periodicals

c) To understand the various reference books

d) To compile a bibliography

e) To locate a specific piece of information

f) For other purposes (Specify....)

2. What is your opinion about the library staff in the university library about the following?

a) Always ready to help

Yes ( )

No ( )

b) Too busy to help

c) Not adequate in number

d) Incompetent to help

3. Have you ever felt that you are not getting the required staff assistance due to inadequacy of library staff

Yes ( )

No ( )

E. Services

1. The following are some of the services rendered to the users by the university library. Do you utilize such services?

Yes ( )

No ( )

i) Reference services ....

ii) Addition list ....

iii) Reprographic services..............................

iv) Interlibrary loan service ....

v) Reservation of books ....

vi) Current awareness services ....

vii) Any other service (specify)........................

2. Do you think that the aforesaid services are adequate for your learning, teaching and research?

   Yes ( )

   No ( )

   If your answer is NO, do you think any of the following services are necessary?(indicate your preferences by 1, 2, 3 etc)

   i) News paper clipping service ....

   ii) SDI ....

   iii) Referral Service.....................................

   iv) Translation service ....

   v) Bibliographical services............................

   vi) Data services ....

   vii) User education......................................

3. Do you think that the present system of manual library operations and services in the university library is time consuming and not very effective?

   Yes ( )

   No ( )

   If your answer is YES, do you think that the use of computers in the university library can improve the situation?

F. Suggestion

Please give your suggestions for eliminating problems relating to the information use and information services in the university library.

....

The designed questionnaires with a covering letter will be administered by the investigator among the population, either the entire population or the sample taken under study. If the informants are not at the reach of the investigator, the questionnaire can be mailed to them. In such a case, in addition to the questionnaire, self addressed stamped cover should also be enclosed. The filled up questionnaires received from the respondents form the base line data for the study.

INTERVIEW METHOD

In simple terms interview means " conversation with a purpose". In the words of Brown and Ghiselli, the term interview stands for a generic concept which includes a variety of procedure used in collecting data through a person to person contact between an interviewer and a respondent. P.V Young defines it " as the very term implies, interviewing is an interaction process, it is a mutual view of each other".

Types of Interview

The interviews can be broadly divided into two types viz structured interview and unstructured interview. The method of collecting information through personal interviews is usually carried out in a structured way As such we call the interviews as structured interviews. Such interviews involve the use of a set of predetermined questions and of highly standardized techniques of recording. Thus the interviewer in a structured interview follows a rigid procedure laid down, asking questions in a form and order prescribed. The unstructured interview is characterized by a flexibility of approach to questioning. This does not follow a system of pre-determined questions and standardized techniques of recording of information. In an unstructured interview, the interviewer is allowed much greater freedom to ask, in case of need, supplementary questions or at times he may omit certain questions if the situation so requires. Unstructured interview demands deep knowledge and skill on the part of the investigator. A model of interview schedule that can be used for interviewing librarians in university libraries is given under

Interview schedule for data collection from Librarians.

1. Name of the university
2. What are the major objectives of the university library?
3. What is your opinion about the provision of space in the university library?
   a) working space for staff
      Adequate ( )
      Inadequate ( )
   b) Working space for users
      If your answer is ' inadequate' suggest approximate area(in sq.feet) required to work the library effectively
4. Do you think the library equipments presently available in the library are adequate to fulfill the objectives of the library.

   If your answer is 'No' please suggest the essential library equipments to be purchased and their approximate cost

Names of equipment/s	cost
i)	....
ii)	....
iii)	....

5. What is your opinion about the adequacy of the following for fulfilling the requirements of the users?

   a) Reading materials

      Adequate ( )

      Inadequate ( )

   b) Staff

   c) Services

6. How do you feel about the present manpower position in the library

   Excess ( )

   Adequate ( )

   Inadequate ( )

7. Have you left out any programme /service during the last 10 years due to lack of staff and finance?

   Yes ( )

   No ( )

8. What type of budgeting technique is followed in the library for the budget preparation

   a) Line budgeting

   b) Programme budgeting

   c) Performance budgeting

   d) Zero budgeting

e) By comparison with past expenditures

f) By using arbitrary standards and norms

g) Any other method

9. Do you think that the present method of budget allocation is adequate to fulfill the objectives of the library?

   Yes ( )

   No ( )

   If your answer is 'No' suggest the approximate adhoc amount required for the following items.

   a) Purchase of books and periodicals

   b) Equipments

   c) Extension of library building

   d) Staff salary

   e) For starting additional services

   f) Stationery

   g) Contingencies.

10. What are your suggestions in order to overcome the problems especially fiscal problems in the university library?

There are other types of interviews such as focused interview, clinical interview and non-directive interview. Focused interview is meant to focus attention on the given experience of the respondent and its effect whereas clinical interview is concerned with broader underlying feelings or motivations or with the course of individual's life experience. In the case of non-directive interview, the interviewer's function is simply to encourage the respondent to talk about the given topic with a bare minimum of direct questioning.

Merits and Demerits of Interview method

There are a number of merits and demerits of interview as a method of data collection. The merits are:

i) There is greater flexibility under this method as there is opportunity to restructure questions;

ii) More information and that too in greater depth can be obtained;

iii) Personal information can as well be obtained easily under this method;

iv) The language of the interview can be adopted to the ability or educational level of the person interviewed and as such misinterpretations concerning questions can be avoided.

The demerits of interview method are:

1. It is an expensive and time consuming method;
2. There remains the possibility of bias of interviewer as well as the respondent;
3. Certain types of respondents such as high officials, executives etc may not be easily approachable for interview;
4. The presence of the interviewer on the spot may over stimulate the respondent, sometimes even to the extent that he may give imaginary information just to make the interview interesting;
5. Interviewing at times may also introduce systematic errors.

OBSERVATION METHOD

Observation is one of the primary data collection methods. This is one of the oldest data collection method which is widely used in social science research. This method has been defined by different schools of thought in different ways. It is an accurate watching and noting of the phenomena as they occur in nature with regard to the cause and effect of mutual relations. It is a data collection method in which a person observes subjects of phenomena and records information about characteristics of the phenomena. Pauline V Young has defined observation as deliberate study through the eye which may be used as one of the methods for scrutinizing collective behaviour and complex of institutions as well as separate units composing of totality. In the words of Busha the term observation is the object or subject of an investigation being subjected to in a situation close - usually visual -surveillance and that the information obtained will then be related to more general propositions or theories. Goode and Hatt state that 'observation may take many forms and is, at once the most primitive and the most modern of research techniques'

Carter V Good and others state the following characteristic features of observation.

i) Observation is specific, not haphazard looking around by general impressions;

ii) Scientific observation of behaviour is systematic not chance dropping in a situation ;

iii) Observation is quantitative recording of the number of instances, certain types of behaviour are noted;

iv) Observation is recorded immediately - notes are made promptly rather than trusting to memory;

v) Observation is expert - being done by some one trained to do such work; and

vi) Observational result can be checked and substantiated to ascertain reliability and validity.

TYPES OF OBSERVATION

Observation can be divided into various types based on applying various characteristics. They are:

a) Controlled observation

The observation that takes place according to definite pre-arranged plans, involving experimental procedure is termed controlled observation. In controlled observation, we use mechanical instruments as aid to accuracy and standardization. Generally controlled observation takes place in various experiments that are carried out in laboratory settings.

b) Uncontrolled observation

If the observation takes place in the natural setting, it may be termed as uncontrolled observation. In uncontrolled observation, no attempt is made to use precision instruments. The major objective of this type of observation is to get a spontaneous picture of the life and activities of the target population. This type of observation is resorted to in the case of exploratory researches.

c) Participant observation

If the observer observes by making himself more or less a member of the group experience, the observation is called participant observation.

d) Non-Participant Observation

When the observer observes as a detached emissary without any attempt on his part to experience through participation what others feel, the observation is termed non-participant observation.

e) Obstructive Observation

It is forward and open.. For example when the

researcher openly examines the functioning of an institution it is obstructive observation.

f) Un-obstructive observation

It is discrete and clandestine in nature. For example when a researcher examines without anyone's knowledge it is un-obstructive observation.

g) Structured observation

It is a formal technique. It is systematic, rigid and of specific nature. This method is generally applicable in field studies and experimental settings.

h) Unstructured observation

In unstructured observation procedure, a researcher does not have a pre-determined set of categories of behavior. It is an informal and relatively flexible type of observation method which is quite useful for exploratory research.

GUIDELINES FOR MAKING OBSERVATION

The following guidelines may be considered by the researchers while making observation.

- Obtain prior knowledge of what to observe
- Examine the general and specific objectives of the research problem to determine what to observe
- Devise a method for recording results
- Establish and define the various levels of proficiency categories, or rating to be used
- Observe carefully and critically
- Rate specific phenomena independently
- Be well acquainted with the recording instrument and the procedure in its use prior to making observation.

RECORDING TECHNIQUES

The following instruments or tools are used for recording the data generated through observation.

- Short hand recording. Note book, diary etc can be used for this purpose
- Still, motion pictures and, video recording instruments
- Sound recording instruments
- Mechanical recording instruments.

Advantages and Disadvantages of Observation Method

The major advantages of observation method are:

a) Subjective bias is eliminated, if observation is done accurately;

b) The information obtained under this method relates to what is currently happening; it is not complicated by either the past behaviour or future intentions or attitudes.; and

c) This method is independent of respondent's willingness to respond and as such is relatively less demanding of active cooperation on the part of respondent as happens to be the case in the questionnaire and interview method.

The demerits or disadvantages of observation include : It is an expensive method; the information provided by this method is very limited and sometimes unforeseen factors may interfere with the observational task.

EXPERIMENTAL METHOD

Experimentation is extensively used as a method of data collection in physical sciences. Its application for data collection is relatively less in Library and Information research. During the 19th century attempts were made by sociologists to evolve a methodology which could be applied to social phenomenon, like the methodology of natural sciences which yield definite and clear-cut results. The solution of the social problem thus started with the experimental method.

THE EXPERIMENTAL METHOD IS BASED ON EXPERIMENTATION

It is an observation under controlled conditions. According to Greenwood an experiment is the proof of a hypothesis which seeks to look up two factors into a casual relationship through the study of contrasting situations which have been controlled on all factors except the one of interest the latter being either the hypothetical case or the hypothetical effect. In other words experimental method is concerned with finding out the casual relationship between two variables - independent and dependent - in the phenomenon under study. The independent variable is introduced, changed withheld or manipulated to study the results or effects on the other (dependent variable) In fact it can be said that an experiment is a situation in which variables are kept under observation and further investigation.

STUDIES IN LIBRARY SCIENCE USED EXPERIMENTAL METHOD

Some of the significant studies in Library and Information Science adopted experimental method as a method of data collection. They are : 'The effectiveness of the approaches to the catalogue arrangement' an experimental study on the format of library catalogue conducted by James Kirkelas; ' Cranefield studies I & II on the relative performance of indexing systems ' conducted at

Cranefield Institute of Technology in UK ; 'Effect of prime display on public library book use' conducted by Herbert Goldher etc.

STEPS IN EXPERIMENTAL TECHNIQUES

The first step in the application of the experimental technique relates to selecting the problem, formulating the specific objective, specify design and method. The hypothesis, at this stage, should be stated explicitly in general terms. The second step consists in setting up the field experiment. The factors to be controlled must be assessed; the cooperation between the researcher and the subject must be set up. The third step is the choice of the experimental design regarding its size, material, control groups etc. The choice of material should be based on the criterion of maximum possible accuracy. The basic problem of design relates to control. Control and experimental groups should be matched on all important factors. Control is necessary to reduce variations. In some experiments, some variables may be eliminated. Undesired variations can be reduced by standardization. A good experiment tries to maximize standardization.

The experimental design or experimental formulation is concerned with finding out the casual relationship between two variables- independent and dependent variables. These experimental design can be broadly divided into the following four categories.

a) After -only or post test only experimental design. This is carried out under the social condition or phenomenon which is not at all under control of the physical or natural condition. The two groups are assumed to be equivalent at the start of a study. The groups may be of similar occupation or similar age.

b) Before -After or Pre test - post test design. In this type of controlled experiment, all the groups are selected, observed and measured before experimentation. In fact, the effect is measured both before and after the exposure of groups to experiment, and one or several groups may be used.

c) Ex-post facto design. In this design, the investigator selects two or more groups. In one group an event has taken place, while in the other an event has not taken place. Through comparative study, the investigator proceeds from the present to the past. Thus, it is experimentation in reverse.

d) Panel study. It is a method of study of a particular subject over -time by using different kinds of data. In the panel technique, the variation in the result may be attributed to a real change in the phenomenon.

MERITS OF EXPERIMENTAL METHOD

The merits of experimental method are:

i) The cause and effect relation is more clearly determined in experimental formulations;

ii) It is more accurate and precise;

iii) It is an ideal method for testing a casual hypothesis;

iv) It is considered the most scientific method.

HISTORICAL METHOD

Historical method is an important method of data collection in research. It is a method of research into the past of a subject or event, through the study of documentary sources. The object of history is to describe past events, to discover the exact situation in which they appeared and the atmosphere and cross purpose which led up to them. The interest of the historian lies in the past. Similar is the object and interest of historical method.

Historical method is sometimes also referred to as 'documentary method' because of its main reliance on documentary sources. Documentary method may however be considered a slight variation of historical method because while historical method is essentially based on documentary sources, documentary method may not essentially be used for the study of the past alone. G.J. Garrghan defines historical method as' systematic body of principles and rules designed to aid effective in gathering some material of history of any discipline, apprising them critically and presenting a synthesis of the results achieved'. In the words of Richard F Clark historical method is 'a system or right procedure for attainment of historical truth' Young defines historical method as 'the induction of principles through research into the past and the social forces which have shaken the present'

Historical method enables us to peep into remote past of human civilization when the society and science were in a much developed stage. It helps us in revealing our cultural, scientific, literal and social heritage. Explaining the significance of historical method Gopal writes ' The past has a great role to play in all societies, but in backward economics, the impact of tradition and social institution on development is all the more important ....the past is often the key to the present for the simple reason that institutions like life, are a growth and not a series of disjoined event and the longer the history, the greater is the influence in a social vacuum..... the past has a casual relation to the present.

STAGES IN HISTORICAL RESEARCH

Historical research follows the following stages

Formulation or identification of the problem

A problem can be formulated in many ways. It may be formed due to interest in the field of study, or the person may disagree on a particular issue with an author or a researcher and may want to undertake a research on the issue

Collection of facts or data

After formulating the problem or after deciding to do research on a particular problem, the investigator proceeds further for collecting facts, data, or information pertaining or relevant to his subject of research. This is a very important stage of historical research. Historical method relies on documentary sources. Documentary sources like primary, secondary and tertiary sources are used as data sources of historical research. Tertiary and secondary sources are important to a researcher since these are the keys to open primary sources. The scholar takes their help to scan and to know in less time and one place as to which of the primary sources are relevant to his research work. A researcher has to rely ultimately on original sources. For data collection the following tips may be considered.

i) Data or information culled out from primary sources only should be relied upon. If a particular information comes to notice after reading a secondary source, it must be verified from the original source

ii) Among many primary source or original sources, preference should be given to the one which is contemporary to the event or nearer in time to the period of the event under investigation.

iii) If information relating to a particular event or person etc is available in many original sources, that information or data which is corroborated by majority of the sources, or at least by more than one source should normally be used;

iv) Data contained in official source, if, any should be preferred to data available in private source.

Interpretation of data

The collected data should be logically arranged, analysed and interpreted for reaching a valid result. In this connection it is pertinent to clarify that interpretation of historical data may also lead to some kind of hypothesis and generalization, but hypothesis and gneralisation in historical method are not exactly what these are in scientific method. In historical method generally we can form judgment instead of generalization. A hypothesis cannot be formed without being acquainted with relevant facts.. Generalisation refers to a scientific law which has proved to be true in past, proved true in the present, and is expected to continue to be proved true in the present, and is expected to continue to be proved true in coming future. It is very specific and not broad. It will be rejected even by a single evidence found against it. On the other hand, historical conclusions are very broad, these may not prove true in all cases and yet cannot be rejected or cannot be termed as false. Historical conclusions are therefore only guidelines and not laws.

Limitations of Historical Method

The following are some limitations of historical method as a method of data collection.

i) Collection of facts relating to very old events is a problem, as sufficient data may not be available in such cases.

ii) Historical events are those taken place in the past. These occur only once and cannot be reproduced or created for experimentation. Hence there is no scope for observation and experimentation

iii) Historical writings may be biased or prejudiced

iv) Repair and face-lifting of historical monuments are carried out from time to time in order to maintain these. This may destroy their historic value and their observation may some time lead to faulty conclusion

v) Invaders and rulers of different dynasties may sometimes change the shape and originality of a monument which may result in a faulty conclusion.

Case Study Method

The case study method is a very popular form of qualitative analysis and involves a careful and complete observation of a social unit, be that unit a person, a family, an institution, a cultural group or even the entire community. It is a comprehensive examination of a single object which may be a group, an institution or a locality taken to be representative of the class. Extensive data are gathered about the individual object selected for study so that what is observed in the representative case is predictably observable in all similar cases. Thus, case study is essentially an intensive investigation of the particular unit under consideration.

In the words of Odum 'The case study method is a technique by which individual factor whether it be an institution or just an episode in the life of an individual or a group is analysed in its relationship to any other in the group'. According to Pauline Young, case study is a method of exploring and analyzing the life of a social unit be it a person, family, an institution, cultural group or even entire community. Burgess has used the words 'the social microscope' for the case study method. Goode and Hatt contend that ' case study is not a specific technique. It is a way of organizing social data so as to preserve the unitary characteristics of social objects being studied. In the words of Stuart A Queen it is 'the examination on a simple situation, person, groups or institution in complex whole, in order to identify types and processes' In short, case study method is a form of qualitative analysis wherein careful and complete observation of an individual or a situation or an institution is done.

CHARACTERISTICS OF CASE STUDY

The important characteristic features of case study method are the following

i) It is a detailed and intensive study

ii) It is continuous in nature

iii) It preserves wholeness of unit

iv) It has completeness of data and is comprehensive in scope

v) There is validity of data inherent in the collection process

vi) It involves confidential recording and scientific synthesis

vii) It results in fruitful hypotheses along with data which may be helpful in testing them.

viii) In respect of the case study method an effort is made to know the mutual interrelationship of causal factors..

STEPS INVOLVED IN CASE STUDY METHOD

The major steps involved in the conduct of case study method are the following.

- Recognition and determination of the status of the phenomenon to be investigated or the unit of study
- Collection of data, examination and history of the given phenomenon

- Diagnosis and identification of causal factors as a basis for remedial or developmental treatment
- Application of remedial measures i.e treatment and therapy
- Follow-up programme to determine the effectiveness of the treatment applied.

ADVANTAGES OF CASE STUDY METHOD

The major advantages of case study method are the following.

i) The case study method enables to understand fully the behaviour pattern of the concerned unit.

ii) It enables the researcher to trace out the natural history of the social unit and its relationship with the social factors and the forces involved in its surrounding environment

iii) Through case study a researcher can obtain a real and enlightened record of personal experiences

iv) It helps in formulating relevant hypothesis

v) It facilitates intensive study of social units

vi) It is beneficial in determining the nature of the units to be studied

vii) It is a means to well understand the past of a social unit because of its emphasis of historical analysis.

viii) It constitutes the perfect type of sociological material as they represent a real record of personal experiences.

DISADVANTAGES OF CASE STUDY METHOD

The commonly cited disadvantages of case study

method are:

- Time consuming and expensive
- At times several studies on a single phenomenon are required before deriving broad principles for universal application
- Because of the use of large group of individuals as subjects, the study at times needs the involvement of more than one investigator
- Because case studies usually employ descriptive techniques, sophisticated statistical analysis is difficult to accomplish.

DELPHI TECHNIQUE

The Delphi method is designed for use in refining judgment data collected from a panel of selected experts. The technique was developed in the early 1950s by the Rand corporation to predict future developments to national defense. Delphi method is a systematic approach to the generation of consensus opinions among a group of carefully selected and anonymous respondents. It is based on the assumption that majority opinions will have greater credibility and authority than the surmise of only the most articulate spokesperson in a group of respondents.

The Delphi method has been widely recognized as a means of supplementing information gleaned from past experiences, historical data or other traditional data sources. One advantage of the technique is its applicability to the collection of information from respondents who possess widely differing views that appear to be irreconcilable. The method is also applicable to interrogations of persons who are widely dispersed geographically.

STEPS OF DELPHI METHOD

The procedures or steps in the application of Delphi method for data collection are the following.

- Select a panel of experts who are capable of providing insightful opinion concerning the pertinent research topic
- Ask each participant to compile a list of value judgments, predictions, or opinions about the assigned issue or topic
- Collect the initial responses and incorporate them into a questionnaire for use in a first round interaction.. Then, request that the same panel members rank the recorded statements according to independently perceived orders of priority or importance.
- Upon receipt of all first- round questionnaires from participants, analyze the data statistically
- Submit the second round instrument to the same panel members, asking them to reconsider their second responses.
- Repeat the above step for the third-round questionnaire interaction. At the conclusion of the third round, the investigator should prepare a final draft of the ranked statements, revealing how much change of opinion has occurred. The consensus opinions should be summarized, together with other pertinent comments elicited from participants.

BRAIN STORMING

Brainstorming is a group creativity technique designed to generate a large number of ideas for the solution to a problem. This method was popularized in the late 1930s by Alex Faickney Osborn, an advertising executive. Although brainstorming has become a popular group technique, researchers have generally failed to find evidence of its effectiveness for enhancing either quantity or quality of ideas generated. Because of such problems as distraction, social loafing, evaluation apprehension, and production blocking, brainstorming method is not more effective than other types of methods.

APPROACH

There are four basic rules in brainstorming. These are intended to reduce the social inhibitions that occur in groups and to stimulate the generation of new ideas. The expected result is a dynamic synergy that will dramatically increase the creativity of the group. The approaches are:

Focus on quantity: This rule is a means of enhancing divergent production, aiming to facilitate problem solving on the basis of the maxim 'quantity breeds quality'. The assumption is that the greater the number of ideas generated, the greater the chance of producing a radical and effective solution.

No criticism: It is often emphasized that in group brainstorming, criticism should be put 'on hold'. Instead of immediately stating what might be wrong with an idea, the participation focuses on extending or adding to it, reserving criticism for a later 'critical stage' of the process. By suspending judgment, one creates a supportive atmosphere where participants feel free to generate unusual ideas.

Unusual Ideas: To get a good and long list of ideas, unusual ideas are welcomed. They may open new ways of thinking and provide better solution than regular ideas. They can be generated by looking from another perspective or setting aside assumption

Combine and Improve ideas: Good ideas can be

combined to form a single very good idea, as suggested by the slogan ' 1 + 1= 3'. This approach is assumed to lead to better and more complete ideas than merely generating new ideas alone.

Steps or Procedures in Brainstorming Method.

The following steps in order are considered for the conduct of the brainstorming method..

i) **Set the problem:** Here the investigator should identify and define the problem. If the problem is too big, the chairman or investigator should divide it into smaller components, each with its own question' Create perfectly definite question.

ii) **Create Invitation and Information Letter:** The background memo is the invitation and informational letter for the participants, containing session name, problem, time, date and place. The problem is described in the form of a question, and some example ideas are given.

iii) **Select Participants:** The chairman composes the brainstorming panel, consisting of the participants and an idea collector Ten or fewer group members are generally more productive than larger groups.

iv) **Create a list of lead questions:** During the brainstorming session the creativity may decrease. At this moment, the chairman should stimulate creativity by suggesting a lead question to answer. It is advised to prepare a list of lead questions before the session starts.

v) **Conduct of the Session.** The chairman leads the brainstorming session with the following activities.

- A warm -up session, to expose novice participants

to the criticism -free environment

- The chairman presents the problem and gives a further explanation if needed
- The chairman asks the brainstorming panel for their ideas
- If no ideas are coming out, the chairman suggests a lead question to encourage creativity
- Every participant presents his or her idea, and the idea collector records them
- If more than one participant has ideas, the chairman lets the most associated idea be presented first
- The participants try to elaborate on the idea, to improve the quality
- When time is up, the chairman organizes the ideas based on the topic goal and encourages discussion. Additional ideas may be generated'
- Ideas are categorized
- The whole list is reviewed to ensure that every one understands the ideas. Duplicate ideas and obviously infeasible solutions are removed.
- The chairman thanks all participants and gives each a token of appreciation.

REFERENCES

1. Busha, C H and Harter, SP(1980) Research methods in librarianship: Techniques and interpretation. New York, Academic Press.
2. Krishan Kumar (1992) Research methods in library and

information science. New Delhi, Hari - Anand publication

3. Powel, Ronald R(1985) Basic research methods in for librarians. New Jersey, Ablex publishing.
4. Sharma, BAV, Ed (1983) Research methods in social sciences. New Delhi, Sterling publishers.
5. Sharma, PSK (1996) Librarians' knowledge of knowledge. New Delhi, ESS ESS
6. Young, PV (1966) Scientific social surveys and research. New Delhi, Pretice -Hall.

8

Report Writing and Evaluation of Research Report

Communication of result through research report is an important aspect of any research activity. Thus while reporting, scholars have scientific obligation to effectively communicate about completed investigation in a comprehensive and accurate manner. The utility of research lies in its wider dissemination and hence it is obligatory for the researchers to communicate their results of research in a systematic manner. The production of meaningful and effective research report depends on the writing skill of the researcher and his ability to use suitable visual techniques.

Research report writing is the culmination of the research investigation. It is at this stage of reporting that the researcher assembles the findings of the study, draws conclusions and evaluates his own findings. Report writing is thus the end product of research activity. Writing a research report is a technical activity which demands all the skills and patience from the researcher. It requires considerable thought, effort, patience and an overall approach to the problem, data, analysis as well as firm control over language and greater objectivity. To write the report, a vast amount of planning and preparation is necessary.

Besides, perfection in the research report can be achieved only by continuous and persistent thought and creative and intelligent writing.

The production of an effective report depends on a combination of factors such as the ability and skill of the investigators for analysis, synthesis and exposition. The major components of effective report writing are the following :

- Selection of an appropriate reader population
- Major components of completed research reports
- Fundamentals of style and grammar; and
- Preparation of manuscripts.

SELECTION OF AN APPROPRIATE POPULATION

A research report is meant for several categories of audiences viz scientists engaged in fundamental research, those engaged in applied research, practitioners, policy makers, funding agencies and the general public. The report should focus on the target audience and include the material of interest to other audience only if it does not interfere with the material required by the specific audience.

MAJOR COMPONENTS OF RESEARCH REPORT

The matter in the research report should be logically arranged. The components should include Preliminaries, the body of the report and auxiliaries in order.

The preliminaries must include the following elements

- Title page should include title of the research topic, statement of submission, Name of the researcher, Name of the research centre, year of submission.
- Preface or foreword, acknowledgement, declaration
- List of tables, List of figures, List of abbreviations
- Table of contents

THE BODY OF THE REPORT

The body of the report should be organized under the following chapters

Chapter I : Introduction

This chapter contains the following elements

- Relevance of the study
- Title, statement of the problem
- Objective of the study
- Methodology/Methodologies
- Hypothesis/ Hypotheses
- Scope and limitations of the study
- Significance of the study
- Organisation of the study

Chapter II Review of related studies

This chapter should contain the review of related previous studies in the field.

Chapter III Background of the study

In this chapter the background information relating to the topic under study should be provided.

Chapter IV. Analysis and Discussion

Analysis and interpretation of the data can be provided in this chapter

Chapter V. Findings and conclusion

This chapter must provide the major findings evolved out from the analysis and interpretation of data

AUXILIARIES

The auxiliaries should include

- Appendix/ Appendices
- Glossary
- Index
- Bibliography. / References

FUNDAMENTALS OF STYLE AND GRAMMAR

A precise and clearly worded research report should be free from grammatical mistakes and must ensure that correct forms of verbs are used, capitalization is used for the first letters of proper names, place names and the first letters of all words in titles of publications excluding words that are articles or conjunctions. Title of books, films, plays and poems should be italicize. To promote unity and logical thought, sentences must contain too many ideas. Simple sentence should be used rather than complex one.

WRITING THE RESEARCH REPORT

Utmost attention should be paid for writing the research report. The report is a communication between the researcher and the reader. The report should be clear, easy to read and accurate in information and statements.

Vagueness and generalization will make the report incomplete. The essence of communication is clarity in presentation. The following points should be borne in mind while writing the research report.

- Clear thinking and clear presentation of the report are important aspect. Poor writing is largely due to hazy thinking. Research report writing is a reasoning process and without clarity of thought, there will not be clarity in writing.
- The researcher should have a good command over language. Too frequently faulty sentence structure, illogical paragraphing, poor punctuation, incorrect spelling and other variations of English usage render an otherwise promising manuscript virtually worthless. The researcher should give importance more to clarity than style.
- One should take care of the economy of words and concentration of ideas and brevity. Repetition and superfluous ness will obstruct the lucidity of the report.
- One should write an unbiased, objective report fortified by facts.
- Colloquial or conversational mode of writing is inappropriate in a research report A thesis should not consist of the reporting of personal experience or opinion but should be critical analysis of the problem
- Readability is another aspect which a researcher should bear in mind. Sentences should not be too complex nor crammed with jargon
- The report should focus on the target audience.

DRAFTING OF THE REPORT

The research report should normally go through three drafts. The objective of the first draft is comprehensiveness and fullness of facts. In the second draft the report should be improved both in the form and the language by considerable trimming and pruning ideas and sentences have to be realigned so that the report gets clarity, order, logic, unity, coherence and naturalness. Presentation of research data in the form of charts, tables graphs, figures enables not only to present the data in a readable form but also helps the reader to understand the more complex tabulations. The final draft should concentrate on the final touches on documentation to make the report authoritative and convincing. References and bibliography would make the citations more authoritative. For the preparation of citations style manuals may be followed. Citations should be consistent and complete in all respects.

EVALUATION OF RESEARCH REPORT

The value of a thesis is determined on the basis of its quality. But, how can the quality be assessed or evaluated since the concept itself is a relative and nebulous one. There is prescribed standard available in the field of research to determine the quality of research. However, some of the guidelines or checklist available to the researchers are those suggested by experts in the field. Of course, the objective evaluation of research reports is very essential for the qualitative improvement of research

GUIDELINES FOR THE EVALUATION OF RESEARCH REPORTS

In their studies Anderson and others have suggested the following guidelines for the evaluation of research studies.

i) Is the problem clearly stated ?

ii) Is the problem significant - will the results contribute to the solution of some practical or theoretical problem?

iii) Are the hypotheses clearly stated?

iv) Are the hypotheses logically deduced from some theory or problem?

v) Is the relationship to previous research studies made clear?

vi) Are the assumptions in the study clearly stated?

vii) Are the limitations of the study stated?

viii) Are important terms in the study defined?

ix) Is the research design fully described?

x) Is the research design appropriate?

xi) Are the population and sample described?

xii) Is the method of sampling appropriate?

xiii) Are the controls described and appropriate?

xiv) Is the research design free of specific weaknesses?

xv) Are the data gathering methods described?

xvi) Are the data gathering methods appropriate?

xvii) Are the data gathering methods properly used?

xviii) Are the validity and reliability of the evidence established?

xix) Are the analysis methods appropriate and are they properly applied?

xx) Are the results of the analysis clearly presented?

xxi) Are the conclusions clearly stated?

xxii) Are the conclusions substantiated by the evidence

presented?

xxiii) Are the generalizations confined to the population from which sample was drawn?

xxiv) Is the report logically organized and clearly written?

xxv) Is the tone of the report impartial and scientific?

Guruswamy and Jayaram in their study entitled 'Evaluation of Research' states that the following guidelines may be used as instrument for evaluating research report. There are nineteen guidelines. The evaluation should concentrate on various elements in the report such as title, prefatory materials included, problem raised, previous studies cited, objectives stated, hypothesis formulated, assumptions made, concepts defined, problem studied, sample design, tools used, procedure followed in research, safeguard taken, evidence presented and analysed, Summary and conclusions, limitations recognized, further works projected, bibliography and appendix and report, format and style used in the report.

In the study 'Methodology of educational research' Koul has suggested twenty one guidelines for the evaluation of research report. In the study entitled ' How to complete your research project successfully' by Judith Bell is given 23 guidelines and in the study 'Research methods in Library and Information science' Krishan Kumar has enumerated a set of criteria for the evaluation of research report.

Busha and Harter in their study have formulated the following guidelines for the objective evaluation of research report.

- What are the conclusions of the research ?
- Does the study answer the research question posed?
- Is the methodology adequate for the research problem under investigation?

- Have the assumptions been explicitly identified and are they reasonable and acceptable?
- Are the instruments or indexes used by the investigator adequate reflections of the conceptual variables of the study?
- If a test or experiment was conducted as a part of the research, are the results sufficiently conclusive so that the hypotheses can be accepted as tentative, and theoretical knowledge or put to practical use?
- Can conclusions of the study be generalized to a larger population?
- Are the conclusions linked to other assertions so that findings can be incorporated into existing theory?
- What is the hypothesis or the research question?
- Is the hypothesis of social or theoretical significance and is the problem stated so that it can be solved?
- What are the independent and dependent variables of the research?
- Do investigators appear to be aware of any intervening variables, and, if so, how did the researchers account for them?
- What are the theoretical implications of research? Does the researcher appear to be aware of them?
- Whether graphical or tabular formats have been appropriately used to display pertinent data?
- If sampling procedures were used, are they adequately explained in the research report?
- If the investigator claims to have selected a random sample, was it actually chosen so that each member of the population had an equal chance of being selected?

- Does the methodology explain in an understandable manner so that it can be easily replicated?
- What techniques were used to analyse quantitative or qualitative data? Were these techniques appropriate for the investigation?
- Did the investigator conduct a literature search prior to project's initiation? If so, is the study then related to past, similar investigations?
- Did the investigator make recommendations for future study?
- Is the research report written in a factual, straight forward, honest and lucid manner, and is it free of incorrect grammar, spelling errors, and emotion laden words and phrases?

Of course guidelines are useful in evaluating a research report scientifically. A research report with good structural organization, objectivity of the content, good visuals and documentation, clarity of language and free from aberrations will be well- rated. The scientific and systematic evaluation of research report will enable to enhance the standard of research output and thereby to make qualitative improvement of research.

REFERENCES

1. Anderson, J(1970) Thesis and assignment writing. New Delhi, Wiley Eastern.
2. Busha, CH and Harter, SP(1980) Research methods in librarianship. New York, Academic Press.
3. Devarajan,G((2002) How to improve quality in research? New Delhi, ESS ESS
4. Koul, L(1997) Methodology of educational research. New Delhi, Vikas.
5. Krishan Kumar(1992) Research methods in Library and Information Science. Har-Anand Publications.

9

How to Write a Project Proposal

INTRODUCTION

A project proposal is one of the media of communication grouped under technical writing. It is considered as blueprint of a research work to be undertaken by a researcher. The success of a research work highly depends on how a project proposal is clearly and objectively delineated. Moreover, the acceptance of the project by the concerned authorities also depends on how judiciously and objectively the proposal is presented. Hence much attention should be bestowed by the investigator while preparing the project proposal. A research proposal may be prepared as part of an academic programme for Master's degree. M.Phil, Ph.D or D.Litt. There is another kind of research, which is carried out by researchers as part of scholarly pursuit, which is not for a degree. This type of research is usually conducted by researchers by utilizing the finance received from internal or external agencies. In the preparation of proposals for both academic and non-academic research programmes the components in the proposal have common features or elements in general. This chapter enumerates the agencies engaged in awarding research project, components of a research project, qualities of a good research project and an example of project proposal.

LEVELS AND AGENCIES OF RESEARCH

A number of agencies are engaged in supporting research project by providing financial assistance .to undertake projects. These agencies include international, national, state and local agencies. The organizations viz UNESCO, UNDP, FAO, WHO, ILO Ford Foundation etc are some of the international agencies engaged in promoting research by providing financial assistance to researches. In India national organizations viz. UGC, CSIR, ICSSR, DST, ICHR, Ministry of Human Resources Development, Raja Ram Mohan Roy Library Foundation etc are some of the major organizations engaged in awarding research projects to researchers. At the state level Department of Science and Technology. Department of Education etc are agencies encouraging research activities. In addition to these agencies, Universities and R and D Organizations at the local level invite research proposals from prospective researchers. In the preparation of proposals for submission to any of the above agencies a number of factors should be considered. These include scope of the agency, thrust areas of research of each agency, guidelines given by each agency in the preparation of projects proposal etc. Most of the agencies have brought out guidelines for the preparation of project proposals. The researcher should follow all these guidelines while preparing the project proposal.

The format of the proposal to be submitted to some of the important funding agencies is detailed below.

The UGC guidelines for submission of project proposal comprise the following components.

(i) Objective of the study

(ii) Justification of the study

(iii) Relevance of an action programme

(iv) Approach and Methodology

(v) Details of data collection and analysis

(vi) Project duration

(vii) Staffing pattern, Budget, and

(viii) Institution's own contribution

The ICSSR has prescribed a format for the submission of research proposals, which should contain the following components.

(i) The title of the project

(ii) Statement of the problem

(iii) Overview of literature

(iv) The conceptual framework

(v) Research questions or Hypotheses

(vi) Converge

(vii) Data collection

(viii) Data processing

(ix) Time Budgeting

(x) Organisational Framework; and

(xi) Cost Estimation

The detailed Information about each component of the above format is given in Appendix-A.

The State Committee on Science, Technology and Environment, Government of Kerala has prescribed a format for the submission of proposals for funded research work.

The proposal should contain the following components of information.

(i) Title of the research proposal

(ii) Broad areas of research

(iii) Project type (Basic Research/ Applied Research/ Developmental/ Demonstration/others)

(iv) Objectives of the project (150 characters)

(v) Applications/Socio-economic importance of the project

(vi) Abstract (300 characters)

(vii) Name of the investigator with bio-data

(viii) Particulars of manpower required

(ix) Particulars of equipments required

(x) Particulars of any other facilities required

(xi) Particulars of the facilities that will be provided by the institution where this project will be implemented, and

(xii) Budget details

ELEMENTS OR COMPONENTS OF A RESEARCH PROPOSAL

The essential Elements or Components required for a typical research proposal to be submitted for research are the following.

(a) Title Page

(b) Abstract

(c) Table of Contents

(d) Introduction

(e) Review of related Studies

(f) Research Design

(g) Analysis of Data

(h) Institutional Infrastructure

(i) Manpower

(j) Budget

(k) Anticipated Results of the study

(l) Timetable

(m) References/Bibliography and Appendices

TITLE PAGE

The title of the research project should be short, clear, properly worded and self-explanatory. Lengthy and fanciful title should be avoided. The title page should also contain the name of the research scholar and the place and name of the institution to which the project work is affiliated.

ABSTRACT

A research proposal should contain an informative abstract consisting of about 200-300 words. It should contain the important elements of the proposals such as relevance, objectives, methodology/ies, hypothesis, data analysis methods, limitations, if any, timetable etc. In the primary selection of a project proposal the abstract will help the expert in the selection procedures without reading the entire project proposal. Hence utmost care should be taken in the preparation of the abstract.

TABLE OF CONTENTS

The major element s of the project proposal should be brought under the table of contents. The various components of the proposal have to be linked with pagination, which will help the experts to verify any component in the proposal with ease.

INTRODUCTION

The Purpose of this component is to introduce the topic to be investigated in all its dimensions. Relevance of the topic of research to be investigated should be emphasized. The general objectives and specific objectives should be clearly drawn. Definition of kernel terms in the title of the research should be given. The significance of the topic in the contemporary research may also be provided. In fact the researcher introduces the topic in such a way as to indicate that the topic selected is so important and worthy to be investigated.

REVIEW OF RELATED STUDIES

As a background of the topic of research a survey of related studies should be given under this head. The objectives, methodology and important findings of the related studies can be provided. The review should be selective and organized in a systematic order. This component will help the researcher in getting a clear idea about the methodology/ies and findings in the similar studies or related studies conducted earlier. The review of related studies will also help the evaluator of the project proposal to understand that the study to be conducted is not a repetitive one but an original one.

RESEARCH DESIGN

Research Design constitutes methodology/ies, hypotheses, testing of hypothesis, Research approach, methods of gathering data, techniques of gathering data and data gathering instruments used in the study. Detailed description about methodology/ies to be adopted in the study should be provided. The methodologies adopted should be suitable to the problem to be studied. Hypothesis should be formulated objectively. The hypothesis should be clear, crisp, short and wise and should be verifiable. The researcher should spell out the research approaches such as historical research, survey research and experimental research and the categories under which the study is to be made. Methods of gathering data, techniques of gathering data and data gathering instruments etc. have to be adequately described in the project proposal. If the study adopts sampling techniques, adequate description of type of sample should be provided.

ANALYSIS OF DATA

The researcher should describe the type of data analysis, which is proposed to be conducted in the proposed study. The data analysis to be conducted manually or by using computers should be described in the project proposal. In case any computer statistical package is intended to be used in the data analysis this has to be mentioned in the proposal.

INSTITUTIONAL INFRASTRUCTURE

The institutional infrastructure is another component, which supports the success of the research project. The institutional facilities such as library, laboratory, computers and space for accommodating project staff in the office etc should be provided.

MANPOWER

In the case of a major project, a number of personnel may be required. In such situation the number of persons required, qualifications of the staff, experience etc should be given in the project proposal.

BUDGET

A statement relating to the expenditure requirement for completing the project work may be given as financial memorandum. Financial memorandum has to be prepared for funded research project. The budget should be a realistic one. Separate statements should be prepared under recurring and non-recurring heads. A typical budget would comprise of the following items.

(i) Salary/Wages

(ii) Stationery and postage

(iii) Printing and Xeroxing charges

(iv) Books and Journals

(v) Rent of building, cost of furniture etc.

(vi) Equipments

(vii) Travelling Allowance

(viii) Computer data analysis charges

(ix) Miscellaneous expenses

(x) Overhead expenditure

ANTICIPATED RESULTS OF THE STUDY

The details relating to the anticipated results from the study may be provided to show the significance of the study. These results may be considered by the funding agency for approving the proposal to conduct the study as a significant one.

LIMITATIONS OF THE STUDY

Limitations, if any, in conducting the investigation by the researcher should be explained objectively. The limitation may be usually in respect of the specificity of the topic of investigation. This will help the researcher to pinpoint the research topic proposed to be undertaken.

TIME TABLE

The project should spell out the time required to complete the proposed project work. The investigator should also propose a timetable to execute various jobs associated with the project work. The break up of time can be considered for the various activities under the heads time required for background work, time required for data collection, time required for data analysis and time required for writing the research report. The timetable for executing various jobs in the proposal will enable the researcher to complete the research work in time.

REFERENCES/BIBLIOGRAPHY AND APPENDICES

References cited in the proposal may be organized at the end of the proposal. The documents consulted for the preparation of the report may also be grouped under bibliography. Appendix/es, if any should also be given at the end of the proposal.

QUALITIES OF A GOOD PROPOSAL

The project proposal as a technical document should have some essential characteristics or attributes and qualities. According to Krishan Kumar the following are some of the features of a good project proposal.

It should

(i) Have an attractive format, free from typographical errors,

(ii) Contain only that information which would enable understanding of the problem and its proposed solution.

(iii) Be precise, well written and easy to understand

(iv) Reflect imagination in research design

(v) Give evidence of clear thinking.

(vi) Show adequate grasp of research and statistical tools applicable to the study.

(vii) Represent a high level of scholarship, giving evidence of deep insight into the problem.

(viii) Be clearly and logically organized, and

(ix) Above all give enough evidence of the application of scientific method of inquiry

A research proposal should be prepared by the researcher with due care. A researcher should be capable of selecting an appropriate topic for the research. A researcher should also take care to structure *i.e.*; the proposal with various components of a research proposal in tune with the guidelines provided by the funding agencies. A research proposal, which is error free and is qualitatively a good one, will be approved for pursuing the research. A model of a project proposal is given as appendix(Appendix B) for potential researchers for the preparation of research project.

APPENDIX -A

ICCSSR GUIDELINES FOR THE FORMULATION OF A RESEARCH PROPOSAL

Project directors are requested to furnish a detailed research proposal covering the statement of the problem, the principal research questions posed or the hypotheses to be tested, if any; the definition of key concepts, the research design including the universe of study, the sampling frame, and type of sampling procedure where applicable; tools to be used in data collection; time schedule; staffing pattern; and an estimate of costs. The proposal should invariably be accompanied with a forwarding letter (in the form prescribed) from the institution.

A research proposal is a sort of a blueprint. Apart from helping the ICSSR to process it quickly, a well-conceived research proposal will later also help in its efficient implementation. Every effort made to formulate a proper research proposal will, therefore, pay rich dividends. Social Science research is characterized by a diversity of theoretical perspectives, substantive orientation methodological strategy, data collection practice and analysis technique. It is, therefore, not possible to indicate in short space all the possible ways in which a research proposal can be framed. However, there are certain characteristics that are common to all research proposals. These characteristics are:

(a) formulation of a problem for research

(b) delimiting the boundary of the proposed research and elaboration of its substantive components.

(c) source and method of data collection; and

(d) data analysis

Given these similar characteristics, individual research proposals will vary greatly in the selection of a researchable problem and the delineation of subsequent steps necessary to complete the research. The selection of a researchable problem depends on the inclination, training and experience of the research scholar. Whatever the problem-and one must take care to see that it is researchable-one of the two primary concerns often underlies a particular research to know and/or to explain particular aspect(s) of social reality. Whether one is motivated by the former or the latter, will have important bearing on how the research proposal is developed and designed. The former objective requires a kind of mapping out operation of usually a segment of social reality in respect of certain of its characteristics supposed to be important. If, on the other hand, the purpose is to explain the occurrence of a particular social phenomenon, the emphasis is on why does that particular phenomenon occur and what factors explain its occurrence either in causal or associational terms. It is obvious, then, that these two types of researches require entirely different strategies.

Whatever the purpose of research, it is apparent that the selection of essential characteristics for either mapping out a particular aspect of social reality or for explaining its occurrence requires the placing of the problem and its dimensions in some context. The context must be provided by the accumulated social science knowledge on the one hand, and the theoretical position one takes in regard to the problem at hand, on the other. As such, a proper research design must start out with formulating a researchable problem and proceed on to locate it in some theoretical perspective and link it up with whatever social science findings exist in the area of enquiry. An overview of pertinent literature in the area of enquiry, therefore, becomes a crucial component of a research design. The purpose of the overview of literature is not to list the number of published, either all or a few well-known works but to cull out important findings that relate to the substantive concern of the proposed research. This culling out of important finding is necessary for determining the salience of the problem itself. On the one hand, and illuminating the theoretical perspective one brings to bear on the problem of research, on the other, thereby helping in the cumulating of social science knowledge.

That there is an intimate relationship between the delineation of theoretical perspective and the overview of literature needs no demonstration. Theoretical perspective informs the overview of literature in terms of selection of scholarly works and of findings in order to illustrate their relevance or insufficiency for the enquiry into the problem at hand. Whether the delineation of theoretical perspective proceeds or follows the overview of literature is a matter of individual preference. However, what must be emphasized here is the necessity of linking up in some meaningful way of the overview of literature and the delineation of theoretical perspective. This is most important since it provides the backdrop for choosing the dimensions that must be explored for a particular enquiry.

Whether it is a descriptive or an explanatory research design, the problem taken up for investigation is invariably rooted in a complex and multifaceted social reality. It is, therefore, necessary to indicate aspects of social reality most relevant for that particular problem. The determination of the appropriate aspects takes its character from the theoretical perspective one adopts. This also describes the boundary of research and provides a basis for ascertaining the nature of data required for the conduct of enquiry.

Usually the determination of the dimensions of a research enterprise is expressed in the language of concepts relating to particular domains of social reality. Since it is a concept or a domain that conjoins theoretical knowledge with empirical reality, it is very important to clearly and precisely define the various concepts or domains proposed to be used in a research project. Also, since a concept or a domain represents an abstraction, the empirical references that constitute that abstraction must be specified. In other words, the concepts and domains have to be operationalized so that the passage between concepts and their empirical referents is made easy and scientifically valid.

While a descriptive research design need not go beyond the delineation of dimensions and their operationalization, explanatory research design must provide additional information on how the explanatory exercise is to be carried out. It should, first, indicate clearly the factors with the help of which one proposes to explain a particular phenomenon and second, enumerate hypothesized relationship among variables. In other words, the proposal must furnish an explanatory model containing variables linked with one another by some kind of interaction supposed to be taking place among them. Thus, the determination of independent and dependent variables and formulation of appropriate hypotheses are the essential characteristics of an explanatory research design.

The next step in a research design consists of the specification of the type of data to be collected, the manner in which they are to be collected and the unit to which they pertain. The data to be collected may, depending upon the nature of problem under investigation, be found almost 'ready-made' in various types of secondary sources or it may have to be generated. In the former case, the sources or required data must be indicated. In the case of the latter, construction of some kind of instrument-questionnaire, schedule, etc, for data gathering becomes necessary. In certain cases data have to be collected through interview, observation or the use of informants. In any case the manner in which data are to be collected must be specified. Also, the unit-individual, aggregate or some other entity about which data are to be collected-should also be indicated. In many cases it is just not possible to cover all the cases of a particular phenomenon even though it may seem desirable. The constraints of time and resources impose the necessity of sleeting a few cases that may be deemed to be representing the entire class. Sampling then becomes an essential part of certain kinds of research design. When sampling is an integral part of a research design, the sampling frame, sampling procedure and sample size must be clearly elaborated and an adequate justification provided for the choice. In certain other cases, especially in respect of case studies or exploratory studies, when the focus of study is just one unit, detailed justification for a particular unit must find a place in the proposal.

When requisite data have finally been gatnered, the data must be recorded in such a fashion that data processing according to some analysis plan becomes easy. It should be pointed out data collected for particular purposes do not exhaust their possibilities when that purpose is served. The data can fruitfully be used by other scholars for secondary analysis, as such the recording of data must provide for the possibility of reuse by others. This is especially true of quantifiable or quantified data which when recorded in a machine-readable form, lend themselves easily to re-analysis. It is, therefore, desirable to put these data in machine-readable form. The proposal should also provide for this and indicate the lines on which data are proposed to be analysed. Specially in the case of an explanatory research design, the analysis plan indicating coding design, the procedure of construction of indices and scales, the use of various statistical techniques for testing the direction and strength of hypothesized relationships, etc. must be included in the research design.

The above discussion suggests that a proper research design should be framed on the basis of the following guidelines, which are only illustrative.

I. The Title of the project

II. Statement of the Problem

In the opening paragraphs of the research proposal, the problem to be investigated should be stated clearly and briefly. The key questions and the location of the problem in the theoretical context of the concerned discipline should be specified. The significance of the problem, the contribution, which the proposed study is expected to make, theory and methodology as well as its practical importance and national relevance should be specifically indicated.

III. Overview of Literature

Summarizing the current status of research in the area, including major findings, the project proposal should clearly demonstrate the relevance of insufficiency of the findings or approaches for the investigation of the problem at hand.

IV. The Conceptual Framework

Given the problem and the theoretical perspective for investigating the problem, the proposal should clearly indicate the concepts to be used and demonstrate their relevance for the study. It should further specify the dimensions of empirical reality that need to be explored for investigating the problem.

V. Research Questions or Hypotheses

Given the conceptual framework and the specification of dimensions, the specific questions to be answered through the proposed research should be sharply formulated.

In the case of an explanatory research design, specification of variables and posting of relationship among them through specific hypotheses must form a part of the research proposal.

VI. Coverage

If in the light of the questions raised or the hypotheses proposed to be tested, sampling becomes necessary, full information on the following points should be given.

1. Universe of study
2. Sampling frame
3. Sampling procedure
4. Units of observation and sampling size.

If the study requires any control groups, these should be specifically mentioned. An explanation of the determination of size and type of sample will also be necessary. Proposals not requiring a sample selection should specify their strategy appropriately and describe the rationale.

VII. Data Collection

The different types of data that are proposed to be gathered should be specifically mentioned.

The sources for each type of data and the tools and techniques that will be used for collecting different types of data should be specified.

For questionnaire or schedule to be used, the following should be indicated.

1. Distribution of questionnaire or schedule in different sections, eg. identification data, socio-economic data, questions on various sub-themes.

2. Approximate number of questions to be asked each respondent.
3. any scaling techniques to be included in the instrument
4. Any projective tests incorporated to the questionnaire/schedule.
5. Approximate time needed per interview.
6. any plans for index-construction.
7. Coding plan (whether the questions and responses will be pre-coded or not, whether the coding is don e for computer, or for hand tabulation)

For interviews, the following details should be given.

1. How they are to be conducted (free associational, non-directive, focused, direct or on telephone).
2. Particular characteristics that interviews must have for the use of observation techniques, described.
3. The type of observation: quasi-participant, non-participant,
4. Units of observation;
5. Whether this will be the only technique or whether other techniques will also be employed.

VIII. Data Processing

The manner in which the different types of data will be processed, the tabulation plan and the types of data that will be processed through the computer should be explained in detail.

IX Time Budgeting

The project should be broken up in suitable stages and the time required for the completion of each stage of work should be specified. For instance, such stages may cover.

1. Preparatory work, including selection and appointment of staff and their training.
2. Pilot study, if any.
3. Drawing of sample.
4. Tool construction (including their pretesting and printing).
5. Data collection.
6. Data processing (which should include coding, editing, sorting, computer analysis).
7. Data analysis
8. Report writing.

X. Organizational Framework

An organizational chart indicating the position, tasks, and number of persons, their level of qualifications/training required to fill the different positions should be given.

XI. Cost Estimation

The cost of the project is to be estimated in terms of total man-months and the facilities needed. Calculate it under the following headings.

(1) Personnel

Position	No. of Person	Salary (Including Allowances, etc.)	Duration	Amount Required
(1)	(2)	(3)	(4)	(5)

2. Travel
3. Data processing
4. Stationery and printing
5. Equipment (total expenditure not to exceed 5 per cent of the total budget)
6. Books, journals, etc. (expenditure not to exceed 5 per cent of the total)
7. Contingency expenses including postage
8. Any other (specify)
9. Overhead charges 5 per cent of the cost (i.e., of the sum of items 1 through 8, where Applicable)
10. Grand total

While suggesting budget estimates for the research proposal the project director should take into account the time, budget, as well as various steps involved in the conduct of the research proposal.

The rationale for the allocation of time and money for the various items of budget estimates must be furnished.

APPENDIX-B

INFORMATION TECHNOLOGY AWARENESS PROGRAMME FOR COLLEGE STUDENTS IN KERALA- A PROPOSAL (PROJECT PROPOSAL SUBMITTED TO THE MINISTRY OF INFORMATION TECHNOLOGY, GOVERNMENT OF INDIA)

Project Director:
Dr. G. Devarajan
Head, Department of Library And Information Science

Project Affiliated:
Department of Library Information Science,
University of Kerala,
Trivandrum-34.

ABSTRACT

Discusses the avenues of information technology in the qualitative improvement of present day education. Emphasise the role of information technology in the effective learning process of students in higher education. Formulates the general and specific objectives of the study. Describes the type of population studied and methodologies followed for the conduct of the study. Discusses the methods and media to be used for the Information Technology awareness programme among students. These include lecture method, and audio-visual methods. Data analysis methods, period of execution of the project, institutional resources and project affiliation, manpower etc. are provided, Detailed budget estimates under non-recurring and recurring heads for a total amount of Rs.29, 85,000/- are proposed for the conduct of the project work.

TABLE OF CONTENTS

INTRODUCTION

The societal development of a nation is highly dependent on the type and quality of education imparted at the various levels. Since education is a specific mode of social practice and collective endeavor made by the society in a particular set of environments, neither its meaning not its form can remain the same for a long time. And when the conditions of our social existence undergo a change, significant shifts in the content and form of education are imperative. A radical transformation in education especially in higher education is called for. In order to bring out such a change the avenues in information technology can be fruitfully utilized in education. The avenues of information technology in disseminating information from the generator to the recipient at a faster rate have high relevance in the qualitative improvement of present day education.

Information technology can play a crucial role in the effective learning process of students engaged in higher education. Today a lot of information is generated through printed media and mass media which has resulted in the phenomenon, "information explosion" or "information flood". This will make the students of higher education meet with a number of problems in making use of available literature in their field of study comprehensively, speedily and with precision. But today because of the progress in information technology a student of higher education can make use of Multimedia, CD-ROM databases, on-line data bases,. INTERNET sources etc. for a voyage from sources that are available in any part of the globe in his/her field of study. But, are they aware of and capable of using the information technology tools to navigate in the sea of information? Are they proficient in navigating subject gateways and Internet tracking? There is lack of awareness to make use of these information technology gadgets especially among students who are studying in the colleges situated in the rural areas. This will lead to underutilization of the information resources, even if I.T. tools are made available in colleges. Hence it is imperative to conduct information technology awareness programmes among college students in the rural sectors to equip them to make use of these tools and resources effectively. It is hoped that this will enable them to overcome quite a lot of problems in learning process confronted by the rural student community when compared to the students in urban areas and also will ensure qualitative learning and quality education in the information age.

The main objective of the programme is to provide awareness programmes in information technology resources and tools to students in colleges especially in rural areas. More specifically the aim of the programme is:

(i) to provide basic information about computer and its

peripherals;

(ii) to introduce various electronic information sources;

(iii) to impart programmes in multimedia information search;

(iv) to introduce students to CD-ROM in various subjects and how to search for these sources, Internet tracking, proficiency in navigating subject gateways; and

(v) to introduce students about IN TERNET sources and impart training in INTERNET and on-line information search programmes.

REVIEW OF LITERATURE

In a study Wood and others report that undergraduate students use computer-based information retrieval services in relation to their cognitive and learning styles. Includes a survey of staff at Sheffield University, UK on their use of computer databases and the extent to which undergraduates are made aware of these services. Results show that only a low percentage of undergraduates use them and there is great variation among students of different faculties. It also shows that, computer assisted learning packages were developed and customized for three departments (1). Charlotte and others in a study point out that the children, mainly 9-14 years old boys use the computer games. The study also points out that quality game and educational programmes are available for use by children (2) Janet Abernethy in a study asserts that as the technological revolution sweeps the country, it is increasingly vital that children become computer literate. Public library has a vital role to play in introducing this technology through the provision of equipment, programmes and elementary instruction to users (3). Wrong in a study traces the development of the national information technology programme for education in Singapore. The study outlines the various developmental stages that cover initiation (before 1990), consolidation (1990-95) and leapfrogging after 1995 where topics like Internet, multimedia, networking, virtual reality and information superhighways are focused upon (4).

THE RESEARCH DESIGN

The Information Technology awareness programme will be confined to college students in Kerala. About 300 colleges affiliated to seven universities are working in Kerala. Of these, about 50% of colleges are located in rural areas. The students in these colleges are the target population of this programme. The awareness programme will be conducted for Degree, post-Graduates and research students. I.T. awareness programmes that are suitable to each level of student community will be conducted separately.

The following methods and media will be used for the programmes

(i) Lecture method

(ii) Audio-visual methods

(iii) Computer assisted teaching

(iv) Distribution of course materials

The above methods/s and media will be used for the programme depending upon the level of students community.

INSTITUTIONAL INFRASTRUCTURE

The institutional infrastructure available in the Department of Library and Information Science, University of Kerala will be utilized for the successful conduct of the project. This project will also be affiliated to the Department of Library and Information Science, University of Kerala.

MANPOWER

The manpower required for the execution of the project includes one Director, one programme Officer, one Audio-visual Operator and one Driver.

Budget

Non-Recurring Expenditure	
Computer (Pentinum III) 64 MB RAM - One (With multimedia kit)	Rs.1,00,000.00
Laser printer - One	Rs. 40,000.00
LCD projector (Colour) - One	Rs. 3,50,000.00
OHP (portable type) - One	Rs. 30,000.00
CD-ROMS, Floppy disks etc.	Rs. 25,000.00
Software packages	Rs. 2,50,000.00
Vehicle (Omni Van) - One	Rs.2,50,000.00
Printing, Stationary and postage	Rs. 50,000.00
Overhead expenditure	Rs. 50,000.00
Total Non-recurring expenditure	Rs. 11,45,000.00
Recurring Expenditure	
Project Director (one)@Rs.15,00pm (1500x12x5) (Honorarium)	Rs. 90,000.00
Programme Officer (One)@Rs.5,000pm (5000x12x5) (Salary)	Rs.1,80,000.00
Audio-visual operator (One)@Rs.3,000pm (3000x12x5) (Salary)	Rs.1,50,000.00
Petrol and other maintenance to vehicle	Rs.1,00,000.00
AMC to PC INTERNET connectivity, repairs of Equipments etc.	Rs. 50,000.00
Vehicle tax	Rs. 20,000.00
Overhead expenditure	Rs. 50,000.00
Total recurring expenditure	Rs.9,40,000.00
Grand total (Non-recurring and Non-recurring expenditure)	Rs.29,85,000.00

ANTICIPATED RESULTS OF THE STUDY

The project will enable to create an information technology awareness among student community in Kerala. This in turn will help the student community to solve a number of problems confronted by them in the field of education.

TIME TABLE

The duration of the project will be five years from the academic year 2001 June to 2006 June. The period of the project can be extended, after evaluation of the five years programme as the second phase of the project.

REFERENCES

1. Krishan Kumar: Research Methods in Library and Information Science, New Delhi, Vikas, 1992.
2. Indian Council of Social Science Research ICSSR research grants. New Delhi, ICSSR, 1999.
3. Kerala, Science and Technology, Dept. Rules for the administration of the research fund, Kerala, Trivandrum, The Govt.1995.
4. Wood, F, et al: Information skills for student centered learning a computer assisted learning approach. British Library research and Innovation Report (37) 1997 P 1-60.
5. White, JA, et al: Accessing ICLAS network log data to study student computer usage, course performance and attitude change. Journal of Information Technology for Teacher Education 3. (1) 1994 P. 79-89.
6. Charlotte, et al: Children gather in the computer workshop Bibliotek. 70(17) 1988 P. 640-41.
7. Abenethy, Janet: Computer literacy and children Canadian Library Journal 41(1) 1984 P. 26-29.

Bibliography

Ackoff, Russell,L. (1953). *The Design of Social Research.* Chicago: University of Chicago Press.

Adams Gerald R. and Schvaneveldt, Jay D. (1985). *Understanding Research Methods.* New York: Longman.

Ahuja, Ram (2001). *Research Methods.* Jaipur: Rawat.

Best, John W and Kahn James, V. (1999). *Research in Education.* 2nd ed. New Delhi: Prentice Hall of India.

Best, John W. (1978). *Research in education* 3rd ed. New Delhi: Prentice-Hall of India,.

Bhandarkar, P.L. (et al) (2003). *Statistical Methods.* New Delhi: Himalaya Publishing House.

Bhandarkar, P.L. and Wilkinson (1998). *Methodology and Techniques of Social Research. Mumbai*: Himalaya.

Bhardwaj, R.S. (1999). *Business Statistics.* New Delhi: Excel Books.

Bryman, Alan (2004). *Social Science Research Methods.* 2nd ed. Mew York: Oxford University Press.

Budhwar, Pawan and Budhwar, Laxmi (2003). *Research Methods for Business Studies: Issues and Perspectives.* New Delhi: Global Business Press.

Burton, Paul (1990). Asking Questions: Questionnaire Design

and Question Pharsing. *In:* Slater, Margaret, (ed). *Research Methods in Library and Information Studies.* London: The Library Association.

Busha, Charles H and Harter, Stephen H (1988). *Research Methods in Librarianship:* Techniques and Interpretations. New York: Academic Press.

Daniels, Robert V. (1996). History. In *Encyclopedia Americana.* Vol.14.Danbury, Connecticut: Grolier.

De Vaus, David (2001). *Research Design in Social Research.* New Delhi: Sage Publications.

De Vaus, David (2001). *Research Design in Social Research.* New Delhi: Sage.

Deep and Deep.

Encyclopedia of Library and Information Science (1978). Ed. By Allen Kent [et al.] *Research Methodology:* V.25. New York: Marcell Dekker.

Fowler, Floyd.J (1987). *Survey Research Methods. Vol.1: Applied Social Research Methods Texts.* New Delhi: Sage Publications.

Gay, L.R. (1981). *Educational Research:* Competencies for Analysis and Application. 2nd ed. Columbas, OH: Charles E. Merrill.

Ghosh B N (1984). *Scientific Method and Social Research.* 2nd ed. Delhi: Sterling.

Goldhor, Herbert (1972). *An Introduction to Scientific Research in Librarianship.* Urbana, IL: University of Illinois, Graduate School of Library Science.

Goldhor, Herbert (2972). *An Introduction to Scientific Research in Librarianship.* Urbana Champaign, IL: University of Illinois Graduate School Library Science.

Good, Carter V and Scates, Doughlas E. (1954). *Methods of Research: Educational, Psychological, Sociological*. New York: Appelton-Century-Crofts, Inc.

Goode, W.J. and Hatt, P.K. (1986). *Methods in Social Science Research*. New Delhi: McGraw Hill.

Goode, William J and Hart, Paul K (1981). Methods of Social Research, London: McGraw Hill.

Goode, William J and Hart, Paul K. (1981). *Methods of Social Research*. London: McGraw Hill.

Goode, William J. and Hatt, Paul K. (1981). *Methods in Social Research*. Auckland: McGraw Hill.

Gopal, M.H. (1994). *An Introduction to Research Procedure in Social Sciences*. Bombay: Asia Publishing House.

Gorman, G.E. and Clayton, Peter (1997). *Qualitative Research for Information Professionals:* A Practical Handbook. London: Library Association Publishing.

Goswami, Inder Mohan, (ed.) (1995). *Research Methodology in Library Science*. New Delhi: Commonwealth.

Griffin, Roger A. (1999) *Using the Internet as a Resource for Historical Research: Prospects and Problems*. (available at http://www.austin.cc.tx.us/history/inres00title.html) (accessed on Dec. 10, 2004).

Handarkar, P.L. and Wilkinson, T.S. (1998). *Methodology and Techniques of Social Sciences:* Mumbai: Himalaya.

Hart, Chris (2005). *Doing your Masters Dissertation*. Delhi: Vistaar.

Hart, Chris (2005). *Doing your Masters Dissertation*. Delhi: Vistaar.

Hawkins, Clifford and Sorgi, Marco (1985). Beralin: Springer-Verlag. *How to Plan, Speak and Write about it*.

Hawkins, Clifford and Sorgi, Marco. *How to Plan, Speak and Write about it?*

Hedrick, Terry E. (1993). *Applied Research Guide.* London: Sage.

Hillway, Tyrus (1964). *Introduction to Research.* 2nd ed. Boston, MA: Houghton, Mifflin.

Isaac, Stephen and William B. Michael (1981). Handbook in Research and Evaluation, 2nd ed. San Diego: CA, Edits Publishers.

Kerlington, Fred. Ed.(1964). *Foundations of Behavioural Research, Educational and Psychological Inquiry.* New York: Rinehart and Winston.

Key, James P. (1997). *Research Design in Occupational Education: Module R11.* (available at www.okstate.edu/org) (accessed on Nov 26, 2004).

Khanna, J.K. (2001). *Handbook of Research in Library and Information Science.*

Kothari, C.R. (1985). *Research Methodology: Methods and Techniques.* New Delhi: Wiley Eastern.

Krishan Kumar (1999). *Research Methods in Library and Information Science.* Edn.2 New Delhi: Har-Anand Publications.

Krishna Swami, O.R. (1993). *Methodology of Research in Social Sciences.* Mumbai: Himalaya.

Kumar, P.S.G. *Research Methods and Statistical Techniques* Delhi: B.R.Publishing, 2004.

Kumar, Ranjit (1999). *Research Methodology: A Step-by-Step Guide for Beginners.* London: Sage Publications.

Line, Maurice, B. (1982). Library Surveys: *An Introduction to their Use, Planning, Procedure and presentation of*

Surveys. 2nd ed. Revised by Sue Stone. London: Clive Bingley.

Losee, Robert M. and Worley, Karen A. (1993). *Research and Evaluation for Information Professionals*. San Diego: Academic Press.

Lundberg, George A. (1942). Social Research. London: Longmans.

Lynch, Mary Jo (ed.) (1990). *Academic Libraries:* Research Perspectives. Chicago:ALA.

Mann, P.H. (1985). *Methods of Social Investigation*. Oxford: Blackwell.

Mann, Thomas (1987). Guide to Research Methods. New York: Oxford University Press.

McClure, Charles R. and Harnon Peter (1991). *Library and Information Science Research:* Perspectives and Strategies for Improvement. Norwood, N.J.: Ablex Publishing.

Mitchell, Mark and Jolley, Janina (1988). *Research Design Explained*. Holt: Rinehart and Winston.

Mouly, George J. (1978). Educational Research: The Art and Science of Investigation. Boston.

Neuman, W. Lawrence (1997). *Social Research Methods*. 3rd ed. Boston: Allyn and Bacon.

Neuman, W.Lawrence (1991). *Social Research Methods: Qualitative and Quantitative Approaches*. 3rd ed. Boston: Allyn and Bacon.

New Delhi: Crest.

Newman, W. Lawrence (1997). *Social Research Methods: Qualitative and Quantitative Approaches*. 3rd ed. Boston: Allyn and Bacon.

O'Leary, Zina (2004). *The Essential Guide to Doing Research.* New Delhi: Vistaar Publications. Pp.150-83.

Partner, Nancy F. (1997), *In Collier's Encyclopedia.* New York: Collier's.

Powell, Ronald R. (1991). Basic Research Methods for Librarians. 2nd ed. Norwood, NJ:Ablex.

Powell, Ronald, R. (1997). *Basic Research Method for Librarians.* 3rd ed. Greenwich: Ablex.

Ranjit Kumar (1999). *Research Methodology: A Step-By-Step Guide for Beginners.* Delhi: Sage.

Sharma, Pandey S.K. *University of Knowledge and Research Methodoly:* Delhi: Ken Publication, 1990.Pp.

Shiflett, Orvin Lee (1984). Clio's Claim: The Role of Historical Research in Library and Information Science. Library *Trends.* 32(4), 385-406.

Simpson, I.S. (1988). *Basic Statistics for Librarians.* London: Library Association.

Singh, S.P. *Research Methods in Social Sciences:* A Manual for Designing Questionnaiares. New Delhi: Kanishka Publishers.

Slater, Margaret (ed). (1990). Research Methods in Library and Information Studies, London: The Library Association.

Thakur, Devendra (1993). *Research Methodology in Social Sciences.* New Delhi:

Thakur, Devendra (1988). *Research Methodology in Social Sciences.* New Delhi: Deep and Deep Publications.

Trochim, William M (2003). 2nd ed. *Research Methods.* New Delhi: Biztantra.

William, Kristy (2000). *Research Methods for Students and*

Professionals. Information Management System. Wagga, NSW, Australia; Charles Strut University.

Williams, Malcolon (1997). Social Survey: Design to Analyse: *In:* Time May *Social Research: Issues, Methods and Process.* 2nd ed. Buckingham, Philadelphia: Open University Press.

Williamson, John B. [et al.]. (1977). *The Research Craft: An Introduction to Social Sciences Methods.* Boston: Little Brown.

Williamson, Kirsty. (2000). Research Methods for Students and Professionals: Information Management and Systems. Wagga Wagga, NSW, (Australia): Charles Sturt University.

Yin, R.K. (1994). Case Study Research: Design and Method. California: Thousand Oaks.

Young, P V (1984). *Scientific Social Surveys and Research.* New Delhi: Prentice Hall of India Ltd.

Young, P V (1984). *Scientific Social Surveys and Research.* New Delhi: Prentice Hall of India Ltd.

Young, P.V. (1988). *Scientific Social Surveys and Research,* Prentice Hall of India: New Delhi.

Young, P.V. (1996). *Scientific Social Surverys and Research.* New Delhi: Prentice-Hall.

Index

M

N

O

P

Q

R